Model
of Incarnate
Love

Model of Incarnate Love

Mary Desolate in the Experience and Thought of Chiara Lubich

Màire O'Byrne

NEW CITY PRESS
Hyde Park, NY

Published in the United States by New City Press
202 Comforter Blvd., Hyde Park, NY 12538
www.newcitypress.com

Cover design by Leandro de Leon

Library of Congress Cataloging-in-Publication Data:

O'Byrne, Maire.
 Model of incarnate love : Mary Desolate in the experience and thought
of Chiara Lubich / Maire O'Byrne.
     p. cm.
 Includes bibliographical references (p.   ).
 ISBN 978-1-56548-378-1 (pbk. : alk. paper) 1. Mary, Blessed Virgin,
Saint—Theology. 2. Lubich, Chiara, 1920-2008.
 3. Focolare Movement. I. Title.
 BT613.O24 2011
 232.91092—dc22   2010050663

Printed in the United States of America

Contents

Introduction

To be human is to seek the meaning of life, to understand its origin, meaning, and ultimate destiny, particularly the mystery of suffering. Christianity grounds its understanding of such questions in a singular event: God's self-revelation in Christ. In his boundless love, Jesus Christ, love incarnate, shows the measure of what it is to be human. And one person best mirrors the meaning of the Christ event — Mary.

Chiara Lubich finds that Mary models every divine activity in the world and every genuine cooperation with it by a creature. As the mother of incarnate love, Mary shows how to love Love and be love, cooperating with God's will in order, by participation, to become "another Jesus."

Chiara Lubich's teaching about spirituality has been acclaimed.[1] But her spiritual experience also has noteworthy implications for theology.[2] *Model of Incarnate Love* explores Lubich's spiritual and theological insight on Mary from one particular vantage point — at the foot of the cross, as Chiara Lubich calls her in that

---

1. See Jesús Castellano Cervera's "Introduction" in *Unity and Jesus Forsaken.*

2. See David L. Schindler's "Introduction" in *An Introduction to the Abba School.*

position, "Mary Desolate." This volume presents only an initial study into one aspect of this profound theme; nevertheless, it does provide a roadmap through Lubich's writings, using a theological lens.

The first chapter outlines the rich theological content of Lubich's experience of God as Love, as well as the complementary themes of unity, and of Jesus crucified and forsaken. The second presents Lubich's understanding of Mary at two moments when she said "yes" to God — at the Annunciation, and at the foot of the cross. The third examines Lubich's understanding of Mary Desolate in anthropological terms — a model of what it is to be human in Christ. It considers Lubich's striking comment that Mary is "the living, most pure and radiant image of God who is love, almost the incarnation of love."[3] The final chapter evaluates the apparent paradoxes within Lubich's theology, Mariology and anthropology through an explanatory scheme that finds the apex of the gospels' logic in the love that Jesus and Mary lived out in the paschal mystery.

This short work, admittedly only an initial exploration, should encourage readers to reflect further on Mary as the one who teaches best how to "complete the 'magnificent journey' planned by God-Love for us: 'from the Trinity to the Trinity.'"[4]

---

3. Chiara Lubich, cited by Marisa Cerini in *God Who Is Love*, p.74.
4. C. Lubich, *A Call To Love*, p.163.

1

The Theology of Chiara Lubich

Introduction

Chiara Lubich's theology is "founded on a uni-trinitarian vision of all reality, on a uni-trinitarian ontology."[1] Because God is Love (see 1 Jn 4:8) and, therefore, one and three, this theology presents itself as a participation in the *perichoretical* relationship that exists between the three divine Persons, each one of whom is the One, because each one is within the other two. Shaped by this reality it is a movement of life that gives birth to a corresponding knowledge.[2]

The Christian mystery contains God, one and three; Christ, the Word incarnate; Mary; the Church; and creation. Each, although distinct from the others, is not separate from them but is contained within and finds its explanation in the other.

Lubich's theology rests upon four cornerstones: "God who is love, unity, Jesus crucified and forsaken,

---

1. Cerini, "The Reality of Mary in Chiara Lubich," p. 20.

2. The value of this movement from life to doctrine is reflected in the documents of Vatican II (cf. DV 8) and by the Orthodox theologian V. Lossky, who maintains that "theology and mysticism support and complete each other" (*The Mystical Theology of the Eastern Church*, pp. 8–9). Karl Rahner notes that "Experience and interpretation form a mutually conditioning unity." See also H. Egan, "A Contemporary Mystical Theology," p. 99.

and Mary."[3] This chapter examines how Lubich's understanding of God-Love informs her theology of unity, then her perception that Jesus crucified and forsaken is the key to this unity. Mary's relationship to these points is examined in chapters three and four.

Having grown up believing that love was one of God's attributes[4] Lubich, prompted by the Holy Spirit, came to realize that "God's very being is love."[5] This discovery revolutionized her belief in an omnipotent God who does not suffer. She came to understand that God, precisely because he is love, abases himself[6] "to the ultimate depths of suffering."[7] This insight, that love is the key to understanding all of God's divine attributes, has guided Lubich's life and the doctrine that has emerged from it.[8]

---

3. Lubich, "In the School of Jesus: Philosophy and Theology" in *Essential Writings*, p. 204.

4. The Old Testament, particularly in Deuteronomy and in the Psalms, contains many expressions about divine attributes. These were revealed in the New Testament in the context of salvation (see Jn 3:16; Eph 2:4). During the patristic period they were thought to be divinely communicated to those who surrendered themselves to God in love.

5. Cerini, *God Who Is Love*, p. 15

6. God, of course, has no gender. In some cases, however, it is almost impossible to discuss the interplay among the three divine persons without using pronouns to avoid awkward repetition. Because Jesus refers to "the Father" and to himself as "the Son," it seems most natural to use masculine pronouns for both of them, as well as for their Spirit.

7. Jean Galot, cited by Rossé in "The Abandonment of Jesus, the Climax of God's Revelation" in *The Cry of Jesus on the Cross*, p. 130.

8. Lubich's discovery of God-Love throws new light on the conflicting theological positions of Scotism with its primacy of love and will, and Thomism with its primacy of knowledge and reason.

Her discovery that "God's very being is love" was immediately intensified with a further insight: "because God is Love, God is One and Triune at the same time: Father, Son and Holy Spirit."[9] Love, therefore, as lived in God's inner self, differentiates while simultaneously uniting. Reflecting on this framework of Lubich's thought, Silvano Cola[10] highlights the difference between the Greek philosophical notion of "substance," which subordinates the parts into the whole, and the Christian concept of Trinitarian love, which "is capable of unifying without confusing, of uniting without abolishing the differences, and of perceiving the relationship of everything with the unity of the whole."[11]

According to Walter Kasper, the scriptural statement "God is love" (1 Jn 4:8) is an ontological announcement that reveals the being most proper to God. Incarnated in Jesus it reveals God's salvific relationship with the whole of humankind.[12] Jesus gives voice to this relationship when he says, "As the Father has loved me so I have loved you" (Jn 15:9). Doing so, he opened the way for human beings to partake in this two-in-one movement towards God and one other in a way that makes it possible to establish mutual relationships of love

9. From an unpublished address by Chiara Lubich upon receiving a doctorate of theology at the University of Santo Tomas, Manila, 1997.

10. Silvano Cola, author of many books and articles, for many years was entrusted with leadership of the Focolare's diocesan priests' branch.

11. Cola, "New Horizons for Theology and Pastoral Ministry," p. 71.

12. See footnote 3 of chapter 4 in Cerini, *God Who Is Love*, p. 83.

similar, in some way, to the love lived within the triune God.[13]

Motivated by their love for God, Lubich and her companions set about putting into practice in their daily lives Jesus' prayer for unity (see Jn 17) and their love for Jesus Forsaken (see Mt 27:46; Mk 15:34). Although distinct, these two moments in Jesus' life are, according to Lubich, inseparably reciprocal. They illustrate the dynamic action of the Spirit of Truth, which is both universalizing and unifying. Like two sides of a coin they reveal that the God who is love in the unity of the Trinity is the same God who became incarnate and died for humankind. According to the late renowned Carmelite and leading expert in spirituality, Jesús Castellano Cervera, these two gospel passages contain universal principles. Those who choose to put them into practice in their daily lives share "in the continuous and luminous transition from suffering to love, in union with the very Spirit of the Crucified-Risen One."[14]

The intimate correlation between Lubich's sapiential penetration and theological knowledge throws light on the mystery of the one and triune God.[15] In

---

13. According to J. D. Zizioulas, God, as Love, "creates an immanent relationship of love *outside Himself*, to an *otherness* of being that is seen as responding and returning to its original cause" (*Being as Communion*, p. 91).

14. Castellano, p. 9.

15. Such "trinitarian logic must in some way be experienced ... to know it; and to guide ourselves towards it" (H. U. von Balthasar, *Theo – logy*/II [Milan: 1990], p. 21, cited by Piero Coda in "A Reflection on the Theology that Arises from the Charism of Unity" in *Nuova umanità* 18/104 [1996/2], p. 158).

Lubich's understanding the Father, in generating the Son, is "lost" in the Son, he lives in him; in a certain sense he makes himself "non-being" out of love and for this very reason he is, he is the Father. The Son, as echo of the Father, returns out of love to the Father, he is "lost" in the Father, he lives in him, in a certain sense he makes himself "non-being" out of love and for this very reason he is, he is the Son. The Holy Spirit, who is the mutual love between the Father and the Son, their bond of unity, in a certain sense also makes himself "non-being" out of love, and for this very reason he is, he is the Holy Spirit.[16]

Since "no one knows the Father except the Son and those to whom the Son chooses to reveal him" (Mt 11:27), Lubich's is a theology "of" Jesus "present in and among theologians."[17] As such, her theology is not a reflection on God "from outside" but one carried out "within" the mystery being considered. It is "a participation, through faith and love, in Jesus' knowledge of the Father."[18] Through the power of the Holy Spirit, those who are "one" in him (see Gal 3:28) receive in all its fullness the knowledge that Jesus gives to his Mystical Body. Her theology recognizes God the Father as the *locus,* Jesus as the method, and the Holy Spirit as the one who guides "into the complete truth" (Jn 16:13). Because Lubich believes that a knowledge of God can be achieved through participation in the life of Jesus, her theology can be

---

16. From an unpublished address by Chiara Lubich upon receiving a doctorate of theology at the University of Santo Tomas, Manila, 1997.

17. Lubich, "In the School of Jesus: Philosophy and Theology" in *Essential Writings*, p. 208.

18. Ibid.

described as a way of "knowing God in God" (see Mt
11:27). Thus it is a way of "being" in God that then blos-
soms into an equivalent knowledge.

Jesus continued to grow in knowledge of the
Father (see Lk 2:52) up to the point when, on the
cross, he experienced himself disunited from his
Father (see Mt 27:46; Mk 15:34).[19] Paradoxically, at
this moment, having entrusted himself to the Father
(see Lk 23:46), he came to know the love of the Father
in the measure and form that the Father had always
known and loved him.

The knowledge that the glorified Jesus has of the
Father is manifested through the Holy Spirit in the
Resurrection. Transmitted in faith, it allows belief in
the words of Paul: "And because you are children,
God has sent the Spirit of his Son into our hearts, cry-
ing, 'Abba! Father!' " (Gal 4:6).

This participative way of knowing entered
creation through the Incarnation, death and Resurrection of Jesus. It is a knowledge simultaneously in the
"not yet," because human beings remain subject to
time and space, yet in the "already," because it can be
experienced to the extent that human beings replace
their individual knowledge with the mind of Christ
(see 1 Cor 2:16).

Jim Gallagher, a biographer of Chiara Lubich,
compares the doctrine that Raymond of Capua[20] drew

---

19. It is possible that Lubich, in moving from one gospel account to
the other, is inspired by the seven words of "the cross tradition."

20. Catherine submitted her illuminations to Raymond, who worked
with her to ensure that her doctrine always remained faithful to
the teaching of the Church.

from Catherine of Siena's spiritual teaching to the work of the interdisciplinary study group, known as the Abba School, which aims at elaborating a theology resulting from the charism of unity.[21] Klaus Hemmerle (1929–1994), bishop of Aachen and noted theologian, contributed greatly to this process. According to him, Chiara Lubich "has conveyed to us a school of life. This school of life, however, is also a school for theology. The result is not so much an improvement of theology, as an original theology that originates from revelation."[22]

Theology and the Charism of Unity

Lubich's theology, precisely because it proceeds from unity, does not exclude other perspectives. Rather, in presupposing and giving value to them, it seeks to integrate them into the one truth that is God, one and three. It does not confine itself within any particular theological discipline but freely passes between ontology, anthropology, spirituality, eschatology, ecclesiology, and mysticism, thus transcending the rigid neo-Scholastic divisions. Lubich's theology is informed by the understanding of a God who "exists trinitarianly, that is differentiating (because he is love and a total gift of himself) into the persons of the Father, the Son and the Spirit … while being at the same time in perfect unity."[23]

---

21. Gallagher, *A Woman's Work: Chiara Lubich*, p. 106.
22. Hemmerle, "Tell me about your God," p. 20. See also *Being One* 11/1 (2002), p. 38.
23. Cerini, *God Who Is Love*, p. 43.

The first point of Lubich's theology, that God who is Love exists trinitarianly, is linked closely with her understanding of the unity Jesus prayed for at the Last Supper. Having instituted the Eucharist and given his disciples the new commandment, he prayed, "that they may all be one. As you, Father are in me and I in you, that they also may be in us, that the world may believe that you sent me" (Jn 17:19–21).[24]

Since Jesus became man "in order to teach us to live according to the model of Trinitarian life, the same life he lives in the bosom of the Father,"[25] Lubich's theology of unity expresses itself in love for Jesus Forsaken who as "the definitive Word of the Father and the apex of Revelation ... lives with unfathomable fullness obedient love for the Father and infinite charity for people."[26]

The constituent elements of Lubich's theology of unity include: Ontology, Theology, the Word of God, the Eucharist, and Jesus in Our Midst. The relationship between her theology and each of these will be considered in the next five sections.

---

24. "The unity Jesus prays for is to be *of the same kind* as that between the Father and the Son — based on reciprocity i.e. a mutual being in each other (Jn 10:38; 14:10). Therefore, just as the Son's being is a being for the Father, and vice-versa, so the being of the individual believers must be a being for each other ... just as the Father loves the Son" (Bultmann, p. 513).

25. Lubich, "In the School of Jesus: Philosophy and Theology" in *Essential Writings*, p. 205.

26. Castellano, p. 18.

Unity and Ontology

The "oneness" Jesus prayed for (see Jn 17) is revealed in the *perichoretic* love of the Father and the Son, the Holy Spirit being "the personal expression of this self-giving, of this being-love."[27] With his very life the incarnate Word of God teaches how to be consumed into one with him and, in him, into the Trinity as sons in the Son.[28] Grace cannot make us become what God is by nature, but grace allows human beings to participate in the divine nature (see 2 Pet 1:4).[29]

Gaudium et spes reinforces this, noting "a certain parallel between the union existing among the divine persons and the union of the sons of God in truth and love … and that man can fully discover his true self only in a sincere giving of himself."[30] According to Karl Rahner, God's ontological self-communication "shares the character of both utter transcendence of the mystery, and of absolute closeness and immediacy."[31]

---

27. John Paul II, *Dominum et vivificantem*, n. 10.

28. J. R. Sachs, p. 27, confirms Lubich's thought: "To be means to live with God, to participate in some way in God's life."

29. In *Mystical Theology: The Science of Love*, p. 230, William Johnson asserts that for John of the Cross this participation takes the form of a spiritual marriage, "which is a total transformation in the Beloved in which each surrenders the entire possession of self to the other with a certain consummation of the union of love. The soul thereby becomes divine, becomes God through participation, insofar as is possible in this life." See John of the Cross: *Spiritual Canticle*, 22, 3.

30. Vatican II, *Gaudium et spes*, n. 24.

31. See *Foundations of Christian Faith: An Introduction to the Idea of Christianity* (London: Darton, Longman and Todd, 1978), p. 129. See also *Lumen gentium*, Chapter One, which cites St. Cyprian of Carthage's definition of the universal Church as "a people brought into unity from the unity of the Father, the Son and the Holy Spirit" (footnote 4).

Jesus' prayer reveals his eternal unity with the Father and his desire that humanity participate in this unity. It also tells us that he, having fulfilled the Law of Moses, now takes the place of this Law by offering himself as both the altar and the victim.[32] In so doing he makes it possible that humanity be united in the Trinity.

Explaining what Lubich means by the nature of unity being revealed in Trinitarian love, theologian David Schindler[33] says "that each of the Divine persons *is* (being) in and through the 'non-being' of giving themselves away to each other. The fullness of each person coincides with the 'self-emptying' entailed in being *wholly for* the other."[34] Although this movement of being/non-being is, in its absolute sense, possible only for God, it does allow us to see that Lubich understands unity not merely in a "moral" or "pious" way but as an experience of being one in Jesus.[35] Her ontological understanding of unity finds an echo in the words of Karl Rahner:

> It must be realized that in earthly man this emptying of self will not be accomplished by practicing pure inwardness, but by real activity which is called humility, service, love of our neighbor, the cross and death. One must descend

---

32. Although John's Gospel makes no reference to the Eucharist, Jesus can be eucharistically understood as both altar and victim.

33. David Schindler, lecturer in Fundamental Theology at the Pontifical John Paul II Institute in Washington, D.C., is editor of the International Catholic Review *Communio*.

34. Schindler, "Introduction" in *An Introduction to the Abba School*, p. 8.

35. Lubich, "For a Philosophy that Stems from Christ," pp. 12–14.

into hell together with Christ; lose one's soul, not directly to the God who is above all names but in the service of one's brethren.[36]

Unity and Theology

Lubich's theology of unity is an intellectual expression of her experience of God-Love, a fusion of love and intelligence brought about through the wound of Jesus' forsakenness. For Lubich this wound is "an infinite void through which God looks upon us: the window of God opened wide onto the world and the window of humanity through which it sees God."[37] He who, out of love, loses the knowledge he has of the Father, makes it possible for us to know the Father in the Spirit and for the Father in the Spirit to know us.[38]

Jesus, in his forsakenness, shows us how to "lose" not only our own thoughts about God but also our very mode of knowing. In "losing" our "human" way of knowing, out of love for God and neighbor, we are made one with Jesus Forsaken. In him we acquire a "divine" way of knowing — with our human intelligence but as "lost" and "found" anew in Christ.[39] Thus

---

36. Cited by Harvey D. Eagan in *What Are They Saying about Mysticism?*, p. 105.

37. Lubich, cited by Coda, "Reflections on Theological Knowledge," p. 49.

38. W. Johnston, in *Mystical Theology: The Science of Love*, p. 22, cites Thomas Aquinas' claim "that while we do not know what God is by reasoning we can know him by love" and that of John of the Cross: "the darkest pages of unknowing are filled with talk of 'loving knowledge.'"

39. Lubich's understanding throws new light on the Western Church's method of acquiring knowledge by study and reasoning, and on the more experiential method of the Eastern Church.

"the true subject of thought" becomes "in the Spirit, the risen Christ who makes us one by gradually stripping" us "of self and so making us sharers in his own thinking."[40] This way of knowing activates the grace of God and makes it possible to say with St. Paul: "we have the mind of Christ" (1 Cor 2:16).

Unity and the Three Communions

Through his death and resurrection Jesus brought about a "new creation" (2 Cor 5:17) making it possible for everyone to experience his living presence. Lubich focuses on three of the many ways to encounter this living presence of Jesus: in the Word of God, in the Eucharist, and when he is in the midst of two or three gathered in his name (see Mt 18:20).

Each of these three ways is, paradoxically, a preparation for and a fulfillment of the other two. Since the Word of God is Jesus "pronounced from eternity by the Father,"[41] it is he who prepares us to receive him in the Eucharist and to have him in our midst. Since the Eucharist is the means by which God nourishes us with his own self, it both helps us put the Word of God into practice and to have him in our midst. Since the spirit of the risen Jesus in our midst christifies us collectively, it enables us to live his Word and to receive him eucharistically. Thus it can be said that Lubich's theology is a way of "knowing God in God

---

40. Coda, "An Intellectual Biography — Klaus Hemmerle's Unique Contribution as a Philosopher and Theologian," p. 11.

41. Lubich, *The Word of Life*, p. 18.

through participation in the life of Jesus Christ,"[42] spiritually present in his Word, in the Eucharist and in the midst of those gathered in his name.[43]

Unity: The Word of God

Chiara Lubich's theology of the Word of God affirms that the Father, in loving the Son from all eternity, generates the Word (see Jn 1:1) "and in turn is loved by him in the steadfastness of the same love, in the Holy Spirit, love which is hypostatic."[44] This internal expression of the triune Love of God precedes and is the basis for an external expression of this same Love. Since "all things came into being" (Jn 1:3) through the Word, the Father joins humanity to himself in his Son, the incarnate Word. "Therefore the very same reciprocity of love, of knowledge, of life that joins the Son to the Father in the Spirit, becomes established … also between the Father and ourselves."[45]

The words spoken by the Word come through the scriptures, which are unique because they transmit life: "When we read Scripture, we make contact with God who is giving us the life contained in the words we are living, those words he originally inspired."[46]

---

42. Coda, "Reflections on Theological Knowledge," p. 39.

43. Vatican II, *Sacrosanctum concilium*, n. 7.

44. Cerini, *God Who Is Love*, p. 24.

45. Cerini, *God Who Is Love*, p. 26. See also Lubich, "When we were living it, it was no longer the 'I' or the 'we' who lived, but the word in me, the word in the group" (*The Word of Life*, p. 29).

46. Foresi, *God Among Men*, pp. 37–38.

These words can strip us of all that is "old" and per-
tains to the "self," and replace it with what is "new"
and concerns the "other."[47] For Lubich, " '[T]o be
Your Word' means to be 'another,' to act the part of
the Other who lives within us; it means finding our
freedom through liberation from ourselves, from our
faults, from our ego."[48]

Being words in the Word means, "He who is
the Word *communicates himself* to our souls. And we
are one with him! Christ is born in us."[49] Therefore,
everyone, regardless of his or her vocation, age,
gender, or social situation, can incarnate the truth
contained in the words of scripture. Putting the words
of scripture into practice brings about a qualitative
transformation in those who live them so that it is
no longer they who live but it is the Word who, as
Love, incarnates itself, expresses itself, and unfolds
itself in a tangible and visible way through all the
dimensions of their human lives.[50] They become
"another Jesus: a living word of God."

Although not always immediately apparent,
the full meaning of the divinely inspired words of
scripture does, through the work of the Holy Spirit,
become clearer with the passing of time. Vatican
II's *Dei Verbum* (Dogmatic Constitution on Divine
Revelation) confirms this: "as the centuries go by the

47. The terminology of "old" and "new" contains an allusion to
    Ephesians 4:22–24 and also to the idea of the "New Covenant."

48. Lubich, *Fragments of Wisdom*, p. 68.

49. Lubich, *The Word of Life*, p. 89.

50. See Lubich, *Fragments of Wisdom*, pp. 67–69.

Church is always advancing towards the plenitude of divine truth, until eventually the words of God are fulfilled in her."[51] By adhering totally to the Word, Mary became what Jesus most characteristically is: Love.[52] She reveals the creaturely way to live the words of life contained in the scriptures and so participate in the eternal life of the triune God.

Unity: The Eucharist

Jesus nourishes through the Eucharist in order to make each person another "Jesus." Since he is substantially present, this sacrament not only provides essential food for spiritual life,[53] but it also unites us with Jesus. For "the sharing in the body and blood of Christ has no other effect than to accomplish our transformation into that which we receive."[54] The assimilation that takes place in the Eucharist, however, is not physical. Instead, given life by the Holy Spirit, we become Jesus in a new and mystical sense. We are made one Body (see 1 Cor 10:17) without losing our creaturely distinction from Jesus and from each other. According to Cyril of Jerusalem we become "participants in

---

51. Vatican II, *Dei verbum*, n. 8.

52. Cerini, *God Who is Love*, p. 74.

53. Thomas Aquinas, *Summa theologiae* III, p. 79, a.1, quoted by Lubich in *The Eucharist*, p. 51.

54. St. Leo, Martyr, Serm. 63, 7: PL 54, 357C, quoted in Vatican II, *Lumen gentium*, n. 26. See also Brendan Leahy's article: "To Live the Life of the Trinity — The Eucharistic Invitation" in *The Furrow* 56 (2005), where, on p. 400, he cites Augustine, Albert the Great, and Cyril of Jerusalem as examples of early Christian writers who believed that in the Eucharist we are transformed into "other Christs."

the divine nature" (2 Pet 1:4).[55] In other words, the
Eucharistic Jesus brings us into the immense and
unconditional love of the Father while simultaneously immersing us in the atmosphere of the Holy
Spirit, whom the Nicene-Constantinopolitan Creed
described as "the Lord, the giver of life."

Corresponding worthily with the gift of God's
self-made present in history through the Eucharist
requires us to abide by the conditions emphasized by
the Church (a tradition stretching back as far as *Didaché*
9, 5 and 14, 1–2).[56] Acknowledging these conditions,
Lubich stresses that the Eucharist, as the sacrament of
unity (see 1 Cor 10:17), requires those who receive it
to live Jesus' new commandment (see Jn 13:34) to the
point where it is no longer individuals who live, but
Christ who lives in them (see Gal 2:20).

"Focused on living the nothingness of self[57] like
Jesus forsaken in order to be totally for God and for
the others,"[58] Chiara Lubich and Igino Giordani[59]
(affectionately known as "Foco" within the Focolare
Movement), one day during the summer of 1949

---

55. Cyril of Jerusalem in *The Later Christian Fathers*, p. 45.

56. *Didaché*, in Library of Christian Classics, Vol. 1 (London: S.C.M.,
    1953), pp. 175 & 178.

57. "In making himself nothing, Jesus forsaken also remains every-
    thing, because he is all Love" (Zanghí, "A Few Notes on Jesus
    Forsaken," p. 11).

58. Cerini, "The Reality of Mary in Chiara Lubich," p. 22.

59. The Honorable Igino Giordani was a political journalist, a re-
    ligious writer and a member of the Italian parliament. Prior to
    meeting Chiara Lubich he had devoted many years to the study
    of scripture, to writing, and to politics, all in an effort to bridge the
    gap between laity and priesthood, matrimony and virginity, the
    sacred and the profane, the world and the Church.

experienced themselves being incorporated into Jesus through the Eucharist. Having received the Eucharist they asked Jesus to "bring about that bond between" them as he saw "it should be."[60] This is how Lubich recalls that experience:

> Foco, enchanted with Catherine of Siena, had throughout his life sought a virgin to follow. Feeling he discovered her among our little group, he approached me one day proposing to make a vow of obedience to me. By doing so, he thought he would be obeying God. In that moment I neither understood the reason for obedience nor for this type of unity among two people. At the same time, however, it seemed to me that Foco was under a grace that shouldn't be lost. So I said to him, "It could really be that what you feel comes from God. Tomorrow in church, then, when I receive Jesus in the eucharist in my heart, as in an empty chalice, I will tell him: 'on my nothingness, make a pact of unity with Jesus in the eucharist in Foco's heart. And bring about that bond between us as you see it should be.' " I then added, "And Foco, you do the same." The following day, after having made this pact, we left the church. Foco had to conduct a conference for the friars there. I felt urged to go back into church. I entered and went before the tabernacle. Wanting to pray to Jesus in the eucharist, I was

---

60. Lubich, cited by Rossé in "The Charism of Unity in the Light of the Mystical Experience of Chiara Lubich," p. 57.

about to call his name, Jesus. But I couldn't.
That Jesus who was in the tabernacle was also
in me. I was still myself, but made another him.
I could not therefore call myself. In that moment
a word spontaneously came from my mouth,
"Father," and I found myself in the bosom of
the Father.[61]

Through a particular grace Lubich and Foco experienced themselves as a single living cell of Christ's
mystical body (see Jn 17 and Gal 2:20). This came to be
known as "The Pact of Unity."[62] With the vision of her
soul Lubich saw the countenance of God "from the
inside" where created beings, made sons in the Son,
made Jesus, can participate in "making themselves
one" with the Trinitarian eternal act of being "consumed" as Love.[63] In other words they experienced

---

61. Lubich cited in Rossé, "The Charism of Unity in the Light of the
    Mystical Experience of Chiara Lubich," pp. 56–57.

62. Following the "Pact of Unity," Igino Giordani's spiritual life
    underwent the following changes: his strong spirituality, which
    had been mainly individualistic, was now expanded through a
    life of communion. He learned how to lose his generous and ro-
    bust will in the will of God. His intellectualism of reason became
    transformed in charity. His ascetic journey discovered the ways
    of mysticism. His love for Jesus crucified was elevated to a love
    for him forsaken. His relationship with Mary was deepened in his
    contemplation of her desolation.

63. While grace does not allow us to become what God is by nature, it
    does allow us to participate in the divine nature (see 2 Pet 1:4). For
    John of the Cross this participation takes the form of a spiritual
    marriage "in which each surrenders the entire possession of self
    to the other with a certain consummation of the union of love.
    The soul thereby becomes divine, becomes God though participa-
    tion, insofar as is possible in this life" (John of the Cross, Spiritual
    Canticle, 22, 3, in W. Johnston, *Mystical Theology: The Science of
    Love*, p. 230).

themselves as being "Jesus, and as him to be in the bosom of the Father."[64]

This event marked a significant deepening of Lubich's mystical experience, a luminous period in the history of the Movement, and a renewal in the life of the Church itself. In this pact, the Eucharist, clearly its foundation, has actualized its potential as the sacrament of the body of Christ: "in its Christological dimension (the presence of Christ in the midst that unites and distinguishes) and in its ecclesial dimension (the community as the body of Christ)."[65]

Biblical scholar Gerard Rossé highlights two characteristics of the Eucharist that come to light in the pact of unity between Lubich and Foco. First the Eucharist, which comes from God through the mediation of the Church, reveals the divine origin of Lubich's experience. "Her human contribution is her total openness that enables Jesus in the Eucharist to express the best of his potential."[66] Second, the ecclesial-communitarian dimension of the Eucharist comes into light in the reciprocal nothingness of the pact of unity. "It is not only bread of life for the individual but sacrament of unity, of Christ's body."[67] The Eucharist, which offers the possibility of being one with Christ

---

64. Chiara Lubich, *The Cry of Jesus Crucified and Forsaken*, p. 60.

65. Lubich cited by Rossé in "The Charism of Unity in the Light of the Mystical Experience of Chiara Lubich," p. 59.

66. Ibid., p. 57.

67. Ibid., p. 58. J. D. Zizioulas says: "No matter how widely something is received in the Church, unless it is received *in the context of the Eucharist* it has not yet been received *ecclesially*" ("The Theological Problem of 'Reception'," p. 191).

and one with each other is, therefore, both the bond of unity and the source of unity.

Unity: Jesus in Our Midst

The words, "For where two or three are gathered in my name, I am there among them" (Mt 18:20), proclaim that the Spirit of the Risen Jesus is dynamically and collectively present among those who, nourished on his Word and on the Eucharist, gather together in his name.

Because these words are found only in Matthew's Gospel they might seem marginal in the New Testament. They continue, however, the Old Testament's covenantal theme of God's relationship with his people: "I will walk among you, and I will be your God, and you shall be my people" (Lev 26:12). This covenantal promise finds its fulfillment in the resurrected Christ who, no longer confined by time and space, is now permanently present not only to the people of Israel but to the whole of humanity (see Mt 28:19–20).

Given that the whole of chapter 18 in Matthew's Gospel is ecclesial, this apparently marginal text (Mt 18:20) has profound significance for the whole body of Christian believers. It expresses the certainty that Jesus, having ascended into heaven, does not distance himself from his followers; instead, he continues to be present, albeit in an invisible way, among those gathered in his name.

He who on the cross made us sharers in the divine life (see 1 Pet 1:3–4) and gave us his Spirit (see Jn 19:30), shows us that his risen presence is not static but relational, a presence that calls us out of ourselves and into unity with him in each neighbor. Although this gospel phrase (see Mt 18:20) was rarely used in Church documents prior to Vatican II, the fundamental idea of Jesus' presence among those gathered in his name appears throughout the Second Vatican Council's documents.[68]

The Conditions for Having Jesus in Our Midst

According to Chiara Lubich, Matthew 18:20 means to be united in God's will which, as Jesus told us, means to "love one another" as he has loved us (see Jn 13:34; 15:12). The distinguishing characteristic of this particular expression of Jesus' presence is its dependence upon fraternal communion, the relationship of unity among human beings. "Only through Christ, who makes persons 'dead to themselves,' and 'alive to grace,' however, is this possible. Therefore, Christ is the one who creates unity and is also its end result."[69]

To love one another reciprocally "as" Jesus loved us requires that the neighbor be seen as the sacrament, the visible sign of God's presence in the world. Jesus confirmed this when he linked the commandment to love God (see Dt 6:5) and the commandment to love one's neighbor (see Lv 19:18). By connecting them, he found a way to assert that whatever we do to the least we do to him (see Mt 25:34–40).

---

68. Vatican II, *Sacrosanctum concilium*, ch. 1, 7; Decree Apostolican actuositatem, ch. 4, 18; Decree Perfectae caritatis, ch. 15; Constitution Lumen gentium, ch. 3.

69. Povilus, p. 61.

To put Jesus' new commandment into practice (see
Jn 13:34; 15:12) means to die to one's own sentiment,
will, and thought, and to allow oneself to be consumed
by the neighbor's sentiment, will and thought (pro-
vided this does not involve sin). Thus, to build communion among our brothers and sisters we must practice
virtues such as poverty, purity, prudence, patience, and
meekness by looking after the weakest in our com-
munities, by not scandalizing, by praying for those in
need, and by exercising unlimited forgiveness.

The Effects of Jesus in Our Midst

Given that Jesus' presence in our midst is spiritual
and not physical, it can only be detected by the senses
of the soul. To recognize and love the living Jesus in
and among fellow human beings requires a readiness
to "lose" self and enter, instead, into neighbors to the
point of being consumed into one with them. This, in
turn, gives birth to a We-community, a new way of being human, a way that defines the heart of Christian
anthropology — as underlined by the Second Vatican
Council,[70] a way revealed by Jesus.

Two or more gathered in the name of Jesus are a
manifestation of the Church, the people of God made
one by Christ. For Chiara Lubich this means that "the
life of the Trinity is no longer lived only in the interior life of the individual person, but it flows freely
among the members of the Mystical Body of Christ."[71]

---

70. Vatican II, *Gaudium et spes*, 22, 24.

71. From an unpublished address by Chiara Lubich upon receiving a
    doctorate of theology at the University of Santo Tomas, Manila, 1997.

Therefore unity, the condition for having the presence of Jesus in our midst, is also the effect of his presence among us.

The Nature of the Presence of Jesus in Our Midst

For Lubich, the presence of Jesus in our midst is both personal and real. It is a reality that those who meet in his name experience in and among themselves: "We are a *single Jesus and we are also distinct:* I (with you in me and Jesus), you (with me in you and Jesus), and Jesus among us in whom there are you and I."[72] This experience of being one and three, of being Jesus individually and collectively, of unity and distinction, allows us, singularly and all together, to say along with Paul: "It is no longer I who live, but it is Christ who lives in me" (Gal 2:20).

Becoming one, each in the other, allows God's idea of what it means to be a person to emerge. Created in the image of the triune God, human beings contain within themselves the paradoxical and simultaneous relationship between "being" and "not being." Activated by grace, this makeup allows them, both individually and collectively, to be "another Jesus" and so to fulfill God's design: "that they may all be one" (Jn 17:21).

Jesus Forsaken

While reading the gospels in the air-raid shelters, Lubich and her friends recognized Jesus' prayer for

---

72. Povilus, p. 62.

unity (see Jn 17:21) as the *magna carta* of the new life
coming to birth around them. Devoting all their ener-
gies to living the Word of God, through whom "all
things came into being" (Jn 1:3), they soon discovered
Jesus Forsaken to be the key, the method, the secret to
achieving this unity.

Through a particular incident on 24 January
1944[73] Lubich, sensing herself guided by the Holy
Spirit, came to understand that the apex of Jesus' suffering occurred on the cross, when he no longer felt
himself united to his Father in the Spirit. She further
understood that his cry of abandonment: "My God,
my God, why have you forsaken me?" (Mk 15:34; Mt
27:46) gave voice to a love that lets itself be torn apart
so that all may be one (see Jn 17).[74]

Jesus Forsaken — the Word of God Fully
   Disclosed

Throughout history God has revealed his identity through his Word (see DV 1–5, 26), through the
prophets (see Heb 1:1; 2 Pet 1:21), by Jesus (see Lk 5:1),
by his apostles (see Acts 13:5; 17:13; 1 Thes 2:13), and
by those who follow them (see 1 Thes 2:9). Written
under the inspiration of the Holy Spirit (see Rom 15:4;
2 Tim 3:16; 2 Pet 1:20–21; see also DV 11), the words of
God speak of a reality simultaneously revealing and
saving (see Rom 1:15–17; 1 Cor 1:18; 2 Cor 2:14–16).

---

73. See footnote 21 in Lubich, *A New Way*, p. 52.

74. Joseph Ratzinger cites Ernst Käsemann's description of Jesus' death-
cry "as a prayer from hell, as the erection of the first commandment
in the wilderness of God's apparent absence" (Ratzinger, p. 226).

This reality became, in "the fullness of time" (Gal 4:4), incarnate and "lived among us" (Jn 1:14).

Jesus brought to earth nothing less than the Trinitarian love of God. Although this mystery cannot be fully expressed in human terms, David Schindler begins to explore it when he says: "divine Trinitarian love finds its decisive expression in the historical economy in the words of Jesus on the cross: 'My God, my God, why have you forsaken me?' (Mk 15:34; Mt 27:46)."[75] This cry, for Lubich, marks the moment when, "in a certain sense he experiences being separated from his Father with whom he is and remains *one*."[76]

Speaking from the experience and theological perspective of the charism of unity, Piero Coda[77] notes that "abandonment is not one particular aspect of Jesus among others; it is the reality that expresses the deepest essence of the event of Jesus himself, and therefore, of the revelation of God and of creation that Jesus himself is."[78] This revelation presents the triune God who, in Jesus, "dies" to himself and makes himself, if it can be so expressed, into a created reality so that this created reality, in him, might "die" to itself and become God by participation.[79] Thus, by being infinitely empty of self,

---

75. Schindler, "Introduction" in An Introduction to the *Abba School*, p. 8.

76. From an unpublished address by Chiara Lubich upon receiving a doctorate of theology at the University of Santo Tomas, Manila, 1997.

77. Piero Coda, who has doctorates in both philosophy and theology, is professor of fundamental theology at the Lateran University in Rome, President of the Italian Theological Association, consultor for the Pontifical Council for Interreligious Dialogue, and a member of the Abba School.

78. Coda, "Reflections on Theological Knowledge," p. 48.

79. See Coda, "A Reflection on the Theology that Arises from the Charism of Unity" in Nuova umanità 104/18 (1996/2), p. 162.

Jesus Forsaken becomes the window through which God looks at humanity and through which human beings can glimpse God. In the words of Hubertus Blaumeiser,[80] Jesus Forsaken is "the open passageway through which the life of the Trinity is communicated to humanity and humanity can enter God."[81] As God, eternally one with the Father and with the Holy Spirit, Jesus did not suffer the abandonment in his divinity. As man, however, he embodied within his humanity "the iniquity of us all" (Is 53:6) and so suffered abandonment in all its intensity.[82] Although veiled by his cry of abandonment, Jesus' humanity was so united to his divinity[83] that he could overcome this immense suffering and offer it to his Father (see Lk 23:46).[84] Surrendering his very being out of love for the Father and humanity, Jesus Forsaken reveals not a non-being that negates Being but the non-

---

80. Hubertus Blaumeiser is currently in charge of the Focolare Movement's diocesan priests' branch and is a member of the Abba School.

81. Blaumeiser, p. 8.

82. The Orthodox theologian Olivier Clément writes: "By his self-abasement, his degradation, his passion, his dying the death of the accursed, Christ accepts into himself all hell, all the death of the fallen world, even the terrible accusation of atheism: 'My God, my God, why hast thou forsaken me?' " (*On Human Being*, p. 146).

83. The union between the full humanity and divinity in the one (divine) person of Jesus Christ, known as the Hypostatic Union, occurred when "the Word became flesh" (Jn 1:14). This doctrine was defined by the Council of Chalcedon in 451.

84. "In that moment everything turns upside down.... The abyss of despair vanishes like an insignificant drop of hatred in an infinite abyss of love. The distance between the Father and the Son is no longer the place of hell, but of the Spirit" (Ecumenical Patriarch Bartholomew of Constantinople, "Commentary on the Way of the Cross at the Colosseum," in *L'Osservatore romano*, 3 April 1994, p. 7).

being that reveals Being as Love.[85] According to Walter
Kasper, God "is himself precisely when he enters into
that which is other than himself.... It is by surrendering
himself that he shows his divinity."[86]

For Lubich, the measure of Jesus' love is manifested
by his handing over to the Father the eternal bond of
unity between them — the Holy Spirit. Sensing himself
without the Spirit, Jesus experiences within his humanity an infinite emptiness. Yet at this precise moment he
fully reveals the identity of God and of every human
being. In the words of Chiara Lubich: "Jesus forsaken,
because he is not, is. We are if we are not."[87]

Jesus Forsaken as the Way or Method of Theology

When Jesus said, "I am the way, and the truth, and
the life. No one comes to the Father except through
me" (Jn 14:6), he was in effect telling his followers that
"the cross is the necessary instrument by which the
divine penetrates the human and (by which) a human
being participates more fully in the life of God."[88] On
the cross Jesus, in his forsakenness, illuminates not
only the mystery of the Trinity but also the mystery of
creation and its vocation to divinization.

---

85. The *Catechism of the Catholic Church* states that "God is the fullness
of Being" (213) and that this fullness of Being is revealed in Jesus as
Love (221).

86. Kasper, p. 83.

87. Lubich, quoted by Coda in "Reflections on Theological Knowledge," p. 51.

88. Lubich, "Jesus Forsaken" in *Essential Writings*, p. 91.

In his forsakenness Jesus stripped himself of his very being. Human beings, however, precisely because they are created and therefore receive their being from God, cannot strip themselves ontologically. What they can do during their pilgrimage of faith is "deny themselves, lose themselves intentionally (on the level of the actions of knowledge and love)."[89] Only in death can a person surrender definitively his or her entire being into the hands of God.

While Lubich understands that the Jesus of history, who now sits at the right hand of his Father in heaven, has no need of our consolation, she also understands that, because his cry of forsakenness can still be heard in every human suffering, he does need our consolation in his mystical body. When asked how finite creatures can console Jesus Forsaken in his mystical body, Lubich replied: "If we are united among ourselves, we will have Him in our midst and the Jesus who will be born of our unity will console our Crucified Love!"[90]

Conclusion

The two central points of Lubich's theology can be considered more as forms of theological knowing than as methodological efforts to know the truth of Revelation. Although systematics and exegesis, moral theology and dogmatics, critical scholarship and

---

89. Coda, "Reflections on Theological Knowledge," p. 52.
90. Lubich, *Unity and Jesus Forsaken*, p. 64.

mysticism remain necessarily distinct, they can all find a new dynamic unity in "the theology of Jesus."

Lubich's theology of unity is an event that occurs in Jesus Forsaken. While God knows things in his triune self, he also knows them in Jesus Forsaken, in whom God and man are united, "without confusion and without separation."[91] He, the Word of God fully displayed, is the way to the Father, a way that enables those united to one another in him to know as God knows. For Lubich, participation in this divine-human knowledge means that every theological reality can be known only insofar as it contains within itself all the others, that is, when it is "in a Trinitarian relation with these others in the light of Jesus forsaken and of unity."[92]

Lubich considers Mary to be the model of Wisdom precisely "because she gave Christ, Incarnate Wisdom, to the world. She did something concrete. It was a deed. Likewise we will have wisdom if we live in such a way as to have Jesus in us and among us, so that his presence will be there in deed."[93]

---

91. Council of Chalcedon (451 AD), DS 302.

92. Coda, "Reflections on Theological Knowledge," p. 54.

93. Lubich, *Being One* 11/1 (2002), p. 18.

2

The Figure of Mary Desolate in the Theology of Chiara Lubich

Introduction

Chiara Lubich's doctrine of Mary Desolate is informed by her insight into the Uni-Trinitarian reality of God. A fundamental aspect of this doctrine is Lubich's placement of Mary within God's plan of love for humanity, fully expressed by Jesus Forsaken and Risen and handed down in the gospels. Called by God into the mystery of his very being, a being that is Love (see 1 Jn 4:8-16), through the power of the Holy Spirit Mary incarnated the Word of God. In her own way she traveled alongside Jesus to the foot of the cross, where she participated in her Son's redemptive work and became "another Jesus." In this way God's design of love for her, and in her the whole of humanity, was completely fulfilled.

Although known by many as Our Lady of Sorrows, for Mary, Lubich uses the title "The Desolate." For her, this name recalls the solitude that Mary "often met in her life, especially at the foot of the cross, solitude in which she always knew how to lose everything in order to make herself one with God's will."[1]

---

1. Lubich, "Mary in the Focolare Movement" in *Essential Writings*, p. 42.

If Mary is the mother of the Word of God and if that Word is "totally revealed in his abandonment,"[2] then Mary Desolate, through her participation in her Son's forsakenness, is that Word fully lived out. Because Mary knew she was totally dependent on her Creator, she knew how to "lose" everything not of him. In conforming her own will to his, she identified with "the gospel's most profound law: knowing how to lose. 'For those who want to save their life will lose it, and those who lose their life for my sake will save it' (Lk 9:24)."[3] Mary's ability to lose everything, including herself, "did not take place only at the last moment of the life of Jesus. She had an intense apprenticeship during the whole of her life."[4] Although conceived free of every trace of sin, Mary remained nonetheless finite and so "always perfectible because the Holy Spirit was growing in her."[5] Mary lived this apprenticeship of ever-growing perfection until, at the foot of the cross, she became "what he most characteristically is: Love."[6]

Contemplating the gospel accounts of Mary's life, Lubich noticed what appear to be successive steps on the road to sanctity. She calls these steps "The

2. Lubich, quoted by Zanghí, "A Few Notes on Jesus Forsaken," p. 90

3. Lubich, "The Charism of Unity and the Media" in *Essential Writings*, p. 299.

4. Lubich, "The Charism of Unity and the Media" in *Essential Writings*, p. 302.

5. Lubich, "Perfect, But Perfectible" in *Mary: The Transparency of God*, p. 92.

6. Cerini, *God Who Is Love*, p. 74.

Way of Mary."[7] Although Lubich does not concern
herself with detailed apocryphal information about
Mary's early life, she does explain how Mary grew up
nourished on the revealed truth of God found in the
sacred scriptures. For her, Mary was "all clothed in the
Word of God,"[8] to the point of being identified with it.

So that Jesus could be the protagonist of salvation for all humanity, God needed a human being to
make a clear choice to open herself up to him. Mary,
who had treasured the Word all her life in her heart
(see Lk 2:19), was the person God asked to conceive,
through the Holy Spirit, that very Word (see Lk 1:35;
Mt 1:18–22). In giving her "yes" to God's will for her,
Mary took the first step in humanity's cooperation
with God's plan of salvation. This new event in her
life was, as von Balthasar reminds us, the first revelation of the triune face of God in human history.[9]

The Annunciation

The angel's words, "Greetings, favored one! The
Lord is with you" (Lk 1:28), set in motion God's gift
of himself to creation and to humanity. Called to be
the mother of the incarnate Word, Mary asked how
this could be since she was a virgin (see Lk 1:34). Told
by the angel that, by the power of the Holy Spirit,

---

7. Lubich, "Mary, the Model of Perfection" in *Mary: The Transparency
   of God*, p. 51. See also "Mary in the Focolare Movement" in *Essential
   Writings*, p. 44. See also *Lumen gentium* 58, which highlights Mary's
   pilgrimage of faith.

8. Lubich, quoted by Cerini in "The Reality of Mary in Chiara Lubich,"
   p. 23.

9. See for example, *Mary for Today*, p. 35, and *Prayer*, pp. 193–95.

the child born to her would be the Son of God (see Lk 1:35), Mary gave her full and free consent with the words, "Here am I, the servant of the Lord; let it be with me according to your word" (Lk 1:38).

At the moment of the Annunciation, God introduced Mary into the depths of the Trinitarian life, into its logic of mutual love. At that moment, according to von Balthasar, God's love "arrived, by way of the Old Testament predilection of the 'chosen,' 'beloved' Israel, to its eschatological end."[10] Mary, in giving her "yes" to God's will for her, became the "you" of God.[11] Her human response to God's divine invitation shows that to be Christian "presupposes both the 'I-Thou' of the Father and the Son within the Godhead in the unity of the Spirit, and the eschatological extension of this to every human 'Thou.' "[12]

Mary's readiness to do whatever God asked of her is an effect of God's unfathomable mercy. While it remains Mary's personal act of freedom, it is both inseparable from and subject to God's gift of grace.[13]

The Visitation

The Gospel of Luke tells us that Mary, having heard her cousin Elizabeth was also with child, set

---

10. Balthasar, *The Glory of the Lord: A Theological Aesthetics VII: Theology: The New Covenant*, p. 439.

11. Lubich, *When Our Love is Charity*, p. 88.

12. Balthasar, *s* VII, p. 441

13. "Speculative attempts to explain how God's absolute freedom in granting grace and anticipating human decisions does not rule out human collaboration and responsibility" (O'Collins and Farrugia, p. 86).

out to help her. Finding Elizabeth open to the mysteries of God, Mary, with a foretaste of eschatological
delight and with the greatest humility (reflecting
her knowledge of her own nothingness and God's
omnipotence), sang the Magnificat (see Lk 1:46–55).
Lubich sees this Theocentric canticle as a testimony
to Mary's being "so nourished by the scriptures that
in her speaking she was accustomed to use its very
same expressions."[14] She further understands it to
express "how Christ, who was already living in her,
gave meaning to past centuries, to the present, and to
centuries to come."[15]

Brendan Leahy, influenced by Lubich's reading
of the story, interprets the words of the Magnificat to
mean that Mary is no longer "outside" of God, but
instead finds herself, if one can say this, alongside
Jesus, turned towards the Father and participating
completely in the mercy of God, which lasts from
generation to generation. According to Leahy, God
looked at Mary (see Lk 1:48) in such a way as to
co-involve her actively in his life; that is to say, he
attracted Mary to himself in order to give himself
to her. From that moment Mary's relationship with
God ceased to be one of "I-God," instead becoming
one of "I and Jesus-God."[16]

The Spirit-enlightened words of the Magnificat
reveal all God has done for Mary, they prophesy "the

14. Lubich, "Mary in the Focolare Movement" in *Essential Writings*,
    p. 40.

15. Lubich, *Mary: The Transparency of God*, pp. 53–54.

16. Leahy, "*Il Dio di Maria*," p. 62.

wonders that God would work through his Son,"[17] and they also tell of the presence of God's Spirit in the midst of human beings (see Lk 17:21; Mt 4:17). Although first pronounced in the context of the Visitation, the Magnificat is an Easter text that projects onto the story of Jesus' conception and birth the glory and power of the Crucified and Risen Christ.

Mary's Divine Motherhood

Since Mary was "only Word of God,"[18] she was able to give life within herself to God's Word. She "kept silent because she was a creature. For nothingness does not speak. But upon that nothingness Jesus spoke and said: himself."[19] With the incarnate Word in her womb, Mary began a partnership with God, thereby becoming "part of the dynamics of the generation of the eternal Word who enters the history of humanity to save it."[20]

Echoing Lubich's thought, Marisa Cerini notes that since the incarnate Word is continuously united to the Father and the Spirit, Mary contains "the Trinity in herself in a singular way."[21] Mary is, therefore, part of a particular *perichoresis* that exists between her individual being and that of the three divine Persons: in her relationship with God the Father, who chose her

17. Lubich, "The Charism of Unity and the Media" in *Essential Writings*, p. 300.

18. Cerini, "The Reality of Mary in Chiara Lubich," p. 23.

19. Lubich, "How Beautiful the Mother" in *Essential Writings*, p. 138.

20. Cerini, "The Reality of Mary in Chiara Lubich," p. 25.

21. Ibid., p. 27.

to be the mother of his divine Son; with Christ her Son, Savior and Redeemer; and with the Holy Spirit who filled her whole existence with his gifts.

The Presentation

Forty days after Jesus' birth, in obedience to the Law of Moses (see Lev 12; Ex 13:12–15), Mary took Jesus to the Temple in Jerusalem, where she met the just and pious Simeon. As the representative of Israel he confirmed Jesus to be the Son of God (see Lk 2:29–30) and told Mary that a sword would pierce her soul (see Lk 2:35). These words, both joyous and sorrowful, characterized Mary's journey towards Calvary and helped prepare her for "the universalization of the Covenant, the Jewish Law, in its expansion through the death of Jesus Christ."[22]

Jesus Lost and Found

Mary and Joseph lost the twelve-year-old Jesus for three days in Jerusalem. When they eventually found him in the Temple, Jesus asked them, "Why were you searching for me? Did you not know that I must be in my Father's house?" (Lk 2:49). This question helped them understand that Jesus' primary duty was to his heavenly Father. For her part, Mary "treasured all these things in her heart" (Lk 2:51).

---

22. Leahy, *The Marian Profile*, p. 88.

The Wedding at Cana

Having lived in Nazareth with Mary and Joseph for many years, Jesus went to a wedding at Cana. In response to his mother saying, "They have no wine" (Jn 2:3), he called her "woman" and asked her, "What concern is that to you and to me?" (Jn 2:5). While the point of this story is clearly Christological, it also serves to show how Mary, by submitting herself to the will of her Son — "Do whatever he tells you" (Jn 2:5) — was being perfected in the wisdom and knowledge of the Holy Spirit.

Jesus, in remaining faithful to the will of his Father, showed that he "could not do anything but the Father's will. He could not do his mother's will unless hers was the identical will of the Father."[23] To be in unity with her Son, therefore, Mary needed to lose her own individual perception of what it meant to be the mother of Jesus and "to become something that belongs only to the Kingdom of Heaven."[24]

Luke does not list Mary (see Lk 8:1–3) among the women who followed and took care of Jesus' needs, nor do the other gospel writers specify how she was contemplatively united to her Son during his three years of public ministry. Nevertheless, it can be assumed that the mother of Jesus had to face an ever-growing separation from him, a separation that reached its peak at the foot of the cross.

---

23. Lubich, *Mary: The Transparency of God*, p. 92.
24. A. Pelli, p. 51.

Mary at the Foot of the Cross

Mary's cooperation with her Son's redemption of humankind began at the Annunciation when, filled with faith and hope, she gave her first "yes" to God. She lived that "yes" in charity throughout her life always trusting in the ongoing self-disclosure of her Son. At the foot of the cross, God asked her to replace the motherhood of his Son with the motherhood of John. Mortifying everything that was human in herself, Mary gave her second "yes" to God and in so doing cooperated fully with God's design of love on the whole of humanity.

At the very moment Mary would have wanted to be closest to her Son — the moment of his death — Jesus entrusted her to John so that, alone, he could offer his life for everyone, including her. Here, according to Lubich, in the "silence of the One replaced by John," Mary experienced "the summit of her suffering, comparable to God's silence in Jesus' forsakenness."[25] Hans Urs von Balthasar resonates with this view when he says that the "women, who in the Synoptic Gospels stand far off from the crucifixion, represent and hint at something that becomes full reality in Mary the mother: accompaniment into the absolute forsakenness, in which, in order to be truly present, she herself must be forsaken by the son: 'Behold your son' (Jn 19:26)."[26]

Whether lost in the crowd or "near the cross" (Jn 19:25), Mary suffered the anguish of not being able to save her Son from his executioners. In "an

---

25. Lubich, *Mary: The Transparency of God*, p. 96.
26. Balthasar, *The Glory of the Lord: A Theological Aesthetics*, p. 197.

abyss of sorrow beyond human endurance, where in her *stabat* she remained standing by a singular grace granted through her lifelong training for that hour,"[27] Mary uttered what Lubich refers to as her second "yes" to God's will for her. With her first "yes" having become the mother of God, Mary, now through her second "yes," gives "back to God the divine maternity that he shared with her"[28] and in the person of John accepts the motherhood of countless human beings. In this way Mary became both victim and "priest";[29] without ceasing to be herself , through the power of the Holy Spirit, she was transformed into Jesus.

In knowing how to lose God (Jesus) for God (in his Mystical Body), Mary participated in a unique way in her Son's redemptive work[30] (see Jn 19:25–27). In so doing she became the first fruit of Jesus Christ's death and resurrection, the first to experience the risen Christ, and the first to participate in the Trinitarian life of communion.

Lubich interprets Jesus' words to his mother, "Woman, here is your son" (Jn 19:26), as entrusting the Church, in the person of John, to Mary. She further interprets Jesus' words to the disciple whom he loved, "Here is your mother" (Jn 19:27), as entrusting Mary to this Church.

---

27. Lubich, "The Charism of Unity and the Media" in *Essential Writings*, p. 302

28. Lubich, *Mary: The Transparency of God*, p. 94.

29. Although clearly not a priest in the sacramental sense, Mary was the first member of the new "royal priesthood," the first person to give her fellow human beings the Body and Blood of Christ.

30. *Lumen gentium*, n. 58, explains that Mary, in freely and lovingly uniting her suffering with that of her Son, shared in a unique way in the redemption of humankind.

Following this line of thought she maintains that the only way to take full advantage of Jesus' words, "And from that hour the disciple took her into his home" (Jn 19:27), is to "take Mary home, and through her, reach Jesus."[31] For Lubich no one explains the Church like Mary and no one explains Mary like the Church.

According to Igino Giordani, the "desolation of the Virgin was the counterpart on the human side (on the part of a woman) of the Son's desolation in the divine when he felt himself abandoned by the Father. The human-divine drama of Mary completed the divine-human drama of Jesus: the single drama of the Redemption."[32]

Mary in the Post-Resurrection Church

In the Cenacle, the upper room traditionally thought to have been the site for the Last Supper, Mary continued to direct her maternal authority towards the apostles. United with her Son's forsakenness through her desolation, Mary, according to Lubich, "no longer 'follows' Jesus: she is now in a certain way transformed into him. Having been conceived in the fullness of grace, Mary was already another Jesus, but now after the descent of the Holy Spirit, the words of Paul are true for her, even more than they were for Paul: 'It is no longer I who live, but Christ who lives in me' (Gal 2:20)."[33] She, who had given birth to Jesus physically, now, together with this post-Easter com-

---

31. Lubich, *Mary: The Transparency of God*, p. 45.

32. Giordani, *Diary of Fire*, p. 53.

33. Lubich, *Mary: The Transparency of God*, p. 65.

munity of believing disciples, gives birth mystically to Jesus present in their midst (see Mt 18:20). Being of one mind and one heart, this group is now the fulfillment of the unity that Jesus had prayed for: "that they may all be one" (Jn 17:21).

Conclusion

Lubich's contemplative use of scripture yields results both profound and dynamic. As well as replicating the Church's traditional teaching on Mary, her understanding of scripture and her reflective theology illuminate some original intuitions on Mary's life, especially her unique relationship with the Trinity.

Through the power of the Holy Spirit Mary was conceived "full of grace," generated the Son of God in the flesh, lived her whole life "magnifying" the greatness of God and his works and, in her desolation, shared in the regeneration of God's children. From her relationship with God who chose her to be the mother of his Son, with Jesus her Son and Savior, and with the Holy Spirit who constantly filled her with the fullness of his gifts, it can be said that Mary, in a certain way, contains the Trinity. From Saint Paul we learn that all are destined to be, as Mary already is, "one" in Christ (see Gal 3:20). The letter to the Colossians (see 1:15–20) extends this vision to all of creation and history. Mary our mother shows us how to be another Jesus and, as him, to be in the bosom of the Father. In other words, Mary models for us how to be inserted into the ever-new and unending life of the triune God and how to live this reality existentially with our fellow human beings.

3

The Figure of Mary Desolate as an Anthropological Model in the Experience and Thought of Chiara Lubich

Introduction

Contemporary theological anthropology has a wide range of meaning and application. It can be summarized as: "an articulation of a vision of human existence within the context of Christian revelation."[1] Although Lubich has not written specifically on the theme of anthropology, her writings have an anthropological tone. She understands God's plan for humanity to be the fulfillment of Jesus' prayer for unity: "that they may all be one. As you, Father, are in me and I am in you, may they also be in us, so that the world may believe that you have sent me" (Jn 17:21). This union with God can be achieved by exercising Jesus' new commandment of mutual love (see Jn 13:34; 15:12) to the letter, i.e., to the point of feeling abandoned by the Father (Mt 27:46; Mk 15:34). When put into practice, these words make God tangibly present in the midst of those who gather in his name (see Mt 18:20). Seen from the perspective of Jesus'

---

1. "Anthropology, Theological" in Michael Downey (ed.), p. 47.

50

prayer for unity, Lubich's anthropology can be seen to be both personal and communitarian.

She bases this understanding of what it is to be human on her discovery of God's very being as love (see Jn 13:34; 15:12), a love lived among the three divine Persons. David Schindler expresses what Lubich means by this: "each of the divine persons *is* (being) in and through the 'non-being' of giving themselves away to each other. The fullness of each person coincides with the 'self-emptying' entailed in being *wholly for* the other."[2] This Trinitarian unity was brought to earth by Jesus who, throughout his life but especially on the cross when he felt himself forsaken by heaven and earth (see Mt 27:46; Mk 15:34), incarnates the measure of love required to redeem humankind, to bring his prayer for full unity with the Father to fruition. He, who paid the price for unity with God and each other, tells human beings that they can have his risen presence among them when they love one another as he has loved them. Marisa Cerini writes that, for Lubich, Mary is the first created being in whom "the trinitarian mystery of God was made manifest for the first time, even though in veiled form."[3] As such she is best suited to show us how "to repeat Christ, the Truth, with the personality given to each by God."[4]

2. Schindler, "Introduction" in *An Introduction to the Abba School*, p. 8.

3. Cerini, *God Who Is Love*, p. 73.

4. Lubich, "Mary in the Focolare Movement" in *Essential Writings*, p. 40.

*Lubich's New Humanism — A Humanism
of Unity Modeled on the Trinity*

Lubich's concept of human existence is based
on the biblical truth that human beings are made in
God's image (see Gn 1:26–27) and that Christ is God's
true image (see Col 1:15). Since the image Christ reflects is "the dynamic relationship that exists among
the three divine Persons, One with the Other, One for
the Other, One in the Other,"[5] each person is called
to cooperate with this gift of God's triune self, made
through Christ in the Spirit. To incarnate this unity is
to enter into Jesus and so "become participants in the
divine nature" (2 Pet 1:4). Reflecting on this reality
Klaus Hemmerle writes:

> the Father, Love, and Jesus, the Son, meet together
> in a Spirit which I would like to define as the
> atmosphere of divine Unity. In this atmosphere
> God opens a space in which I too can enter
> and experience the living God. I am loved and
> embraced by the Father. I am the son introduced
> into the Father. The Father himself has opened his
> infinite bosom, so that I can live in him. Therefore,
> already here in this life I have my dwelling in the
> Trinitarian God."[6]

Hemmerle's experience serves to highlight an
anthropology that contains within it this realization:
"that if the Trinity is in me and in you, then the Trinity

---

5. Lubich, "In the School of Jesus: Philosophy and Theology" in
Essential Writings, p. 212.

6. Hemmerle, "Tell me about your God," p. 17.

is among us, we are in a trinitarian relationship and so our relationship is like the Trinity, indeed it is the Trinity who lives in us this relationship."[7] This biblical and eschatological perspective reveals true being as resurrected and fully deployed in the Risen Son.

The Holy Spirit living within and in the midst of the community (see Mt 18:20), urges them to mirror their lives on the Trinitarian relationships of love and, shaping them from within, enlightens them how to love the other with the measure of Jesus' love (see Mt 27:46; Mk 15:34). The Holy Spirit's guidance, when put into practice — that is, when fellow human beings love one another according to the heart of God — brings about a "new" people in Christ (see 2 Cor 5:17). Each person loves the "you" of the other, "becomes" the other in the unity of the Body of Christ. Lubich's new humanism, which throws light on what it means to be an individual subject as well as on the collective dimensions of human existence, reveals how to "become more Christ, more truly human."[8] As a model of this new humanism Mary, beloved daughter of the Father, Mother of the Son and temple of the Holy Spirit, fulfills God's design of love on her and, in her, on the whole of humanity.

---

7. See footnote 1 in Lubich, "Collective Spirituality and its Instruments," p. 17.

8. Lubich, "A Spirituality of Communion" in *Essential Writings*, p. 30.

The Key to This New Humanism:
Jesus Forsaken

Jesus, by going "outside" of his Trinitarian relationship of Love and plunging into the depths of humanity's consciousness, which had "closed itself off from the Absolute Being,"[9] effected for human beings union with God and each other. He, the true image of God, made this God-less experience his own (see Gal 3:12; 2 Cor 5:21) by giving his physical life (the crucifixion) and his spiritual life (the forsakenness) for humankind. Saved in Christ through faith (Rom 3:21–26; 4:13-16, 25; Eph 2:5–8), human beings have been brought into a new and undeserved relationship with their Creator whereby their nature has been transformed. Through the gift of God's relational life within them, human beings have been made capable of going "outside" their own absolute sense of self and replacing it with a self-emptying love for God and neighbor. This amazing gift brings about a unity between opposites: I-you, me-us, women-men, God-humanity, autonomy-heteronomy, mystical and everyday life, action-contemplation. It is nothing other than a foretaste, already here on earth, of Paradise.

To realize this new way of being human, to become (by participation) God, who is Love, requires continual effort. Jesus Forsaken, present in everyone who is suffering, must be "embraced, hugged to oneself, chosen as our one and only all, consumed with us

---

9. Lubich, "In the School of Jesus: Philosophy and Theology" in *Essential Writings*, p. 211.

in one, while we are consumed in one with Him, and are turned into suffering with Him who is Suffering."[10]

Mary: Model of Union with God through His Words

Mary who, through the Holy Spirit, conceived, gave birth, and followed the Word of God faithfully from Nazareth to Calvary, models how created beings can imitate Jesus Forsaken and, in him, find the direct road to union with God. As the genealogy of Matthew explains (see 1:1–17), Mary was born into the Jewish faith of first-century Palestine and grew up surrounded by God's chosen people. From Abraham she would have learned how to submit her intellect and will in obedience to God's revelatory words. Her vibrant and self-abandoning faith shows her to be a courageous woman who trustingly believes in God as the ultimate truth, as the one who guarantees the promises made in the scriptures.[11] Because Mary believed in God's words (see Lk 1:45), she knew how to listen to them spoken to her through the prophets, to treasure them in her heart, to meditate on them, and to put them into practice during her daily life. Through her reading and prayerful meditation of the scriptures, Mary models how to respond to God's word with a "listening heart," how to be alone with God, to close the shutters of the soul to the outside world, to overcome all the obstacles thrown up by

10. Lubich, *Unity and Jesus Forsaken*, p. 71.

11. See *The Catechism of the Catholic Church*, n. 144.

internal and external conditionings, and so how "to stay mindful and to live the presence of God in us."[12] She also teaches how to align self with the will of God, "to concentrate all our attention outside of ourselves, as when there is a neighbor to love or some task to accomplish."[13] By knowing how to contemplate God's words within herself and to put these words into practice, Mary demonstrates how to balance inner union with God and its external expression.

The personal unity with God that the words of scripture brought about in Mary's soul presuppose a life lived with the most heroic humility, a life that knew how to put into practice the gospel's most profound law: knowing how to lose. "For those who want to save their life will lose it, and those who lose their life for my sake will save it" (Lk 9:24). In modeling how to "overcome the sense of fragmentation that people often experience in relation to themselves, to others, to society, and to God,"[14] Mary manifests how to conform one's life to the plan God has always had for it. In other words, she demonstrates how to generate unity within as well as with God and one's fellow human beings.

Mary: Model of Spousal Union with God

Having previously communicated himself through the created world (see Ps 19:2; Ws 13:1–9), words (see Jer 23:18, 22), and events (see Ex 15: 1–21), God now offers himself to humanity in Jesus Christ,

---

12. Lubich, "The Word That Gives Life" in *Essential Writings*, p. 123.

13. Ibid.

14. Lubich, "A Doctorate in Education," p. 12.

through Mary, as Love (see 1 Jn 4:7–10, 16). She, into whose womb God empties himself (see Phil 2:7), consents to the divine plan at the Annunciation (see Lk 1:26–38) thereby embodying the transition between God's Covenant with Abraham (see Gn 15:18; 17:1–22) and the covenant that would be sealed by her Son (see Lk 22:20; 1 Cor 11:25; Heb 7:22; 8:8-13). The scriptural account of Luke, presented with a different emphasis by Matthew (see 1:18–25), reveals Mary as the anthropological condition of the triune God's advent among us as well as the historic-salvific model of the creaturely response to the creator's revelation.

Having first conceived the Word in spirit, by living in obedience to God's words spoken through the scriptures, Mary now, "with the same docility that is typical of a love which is always gift of self,"[15] set aside her own thoughts and plans and, as the synthesis of the entire creation, presented herself as spouse to its creator. By knowing how to cede her freedom to the one who gave it to her, Mary models how human beings, as children of God, can best realize their enormous gift of freedom. Like her they can accept the all-seeing and merciful plans of the creator and, with a firm resolve, commit themselves to do nothing other than his will.

Although Mary may have thought God was asking her to renounce her virginity in order to become the mother of his Son, she placed her trust in his omnipotence and said: "Here am I, the servant of the Lord; let it be with me according to your word" (Lk 1:38). Through this dynamic hope-filled faith

---

15. Cerini, "The Reality of Mary in Chiara Lubich," p. 25.

response, made possible by her singular cooperation with the action of the Holy Spirit on her, Mary shows all Christians who hope and believe in God that "love is a Someone: it is not just an act of the will."[16] In her relationship with the one she loved the most, Mary shows how to be oriented entirely toward the person of God so that his "will may be done on earth as it is in heaven." God's immense love for Mary, which freed her from conditionings that were not essential to her nature, enabled her to offer herself as a servant of love to Love. Since "virgins are only such if their life is God alone,"[17] this means that those who love, who through the complete gift of self can spiritually generate another life, epitomize virginity's spiritual and anthropological dimensions and anticipate already here on earth the life they shall live in heaven.

Mary's "yes" brings her into "contact with the supreme intelligence that is God." Through this dependence-convergence relationship she exemplifies "the highest possible act of intelligence" as well as "the most effective way of maintaining and extending personal freedom to a divine level."[18] In bringing the religious story of humankind to its climax, Mary shows how every person can have "a direct, personal relationship with God, a relationship of knowledge, love, friendship, and communion."[19]

---

16. Lubich, "A God Who Is Love" in *Essential Writings*, p. 57.
17. Lubich, "Church as Communion" in *Essential Writings*, p. 118.
18. Foresi, *Being One* 11/1 (2002), p. 3.
19. Lubich, *A Call to Love*, p. 12.

Mary's first "yes," her response of faith to God's[20] action in her, brings with it a consequence. She, and those who model themselves on her, now begin the journey that will open them up to God's action in others. This journey will bring them, through their attentive love to the needs of each and every brother or sister they meet along the way, into an ever-greater union with God and each other until, on Calvary, their love will be perfected in unity.

Mary: Model of a Collective Spirituality

Having put herself totally at the service of God, Mary's openness to others begins when she goes to help her cousin Elizabeth, who was with child. Mary, who knew and desired only what God wanted her to know and desire in that moment, demonstrates how to grow in contemplative union with God and so how to participate in God's plan of love. By visiting her cousin, Mary put her love for God and neighbor (see Dt 6:5; Lv 19:18) into action. The initiative for every act of love belongs always and only to God; Mary's grace-filled response, however, shows her fellow creatures how to contribute their free will in concrete acts of service and so how to experience the meaning and goal of personal freedom and identity. Urged to bring the lifeblood of heaven that flowed within her (Jesus in her womb) into the humanity of her cousin's life, Mary's faith gained new vigor which, in turn, reinforced her charity. While strengthening her interior unity with God, Mary's exterior unity with

---

20. Lubich, "Church as Communion" in *Essential Writings*, p. 116.

Elizabeth and "the child in her cousin's womb" was also reinforced. As an instrument of genuine service to her cousin she shows how to generate communion, an oasis of the supernatural in this world. In telling Elizabeth of her spiritual experience, of God's advent among us, Mary's use of scripture, to highlight God's interventions in humanity's past, present, and future, shows her to be characterized by the Word of God (see Lk 1:46–55). These words proclaim her to be exalted in her lowliness and projected into a new communion with "all generations."

As a "clear reflection of the Logos-Word,"[21] she prophesies about the wonders God will work through his Son. As such this unique creature, chosen by God to bring his Son into the world, proves that the Word is not "something outside of us" but is, as von Balthasar wrote, "the deepest mystery at the center of our being, the mystery in which we 'live, and move and have our being' (Acts 17:28)."[22]

The gospel story shows how Mary's faith-filled words fell on "the fertile soil" of her cousin's soul (see Lk 1:41–45). Their hearts filled with love for God and one another, at their meeting these two women each freely chose to "lose" her individuality and, in so doing, "find" herself in the other. Through her respect for Elizabeth, Mary shows how to confirm the other as a distinct, equal, and transcendent being and so how to live the unity in distinction that stands at the center of Lubich's anthropology.

---

21. Cerini, "The Reality of Mary in Chiara Lubich," p. 24.
22. Ibid.

Mary: Model of Maternity

God, in his boundless love for humanity, makes Mary capable of conceiving within her humanity the creative, redemptive and sanctifying God, so making her "the way by which the Trinity comes to establish its presence among us."[23] With all her spiritual energy and physical powers focused on God, Mary "makes herself completely nothing, moment by moment, to give life to him."[24] In giving birth to her divine Son, Mary's faith in God becomes a visible reality, a reality that sees her incarnating the "as" of Jesus' prayer to the Father before his passion (see Jn 17:23) whereby she "is loved by the Father *as* Jesus is loved."[25] Since Jesus is always united to the Father and the Spirit, Mary's divine maternity means she is not only contained within the Trinity but she actually contains "the Trinity in herself in a singular way."[26]

In her role as mother, Mary may have felt that Jesus on occasion treated her harshly as, for example, when she and Joseph "lost" him for three days (see Lk 2:41–51), at the wedding feast in Cana (see Jn 2:1–11) or, when told that his mother and brothers were outside the door and wanting to speak to him, he replied that his mother and his brothers are those who do the will of his Father (see Mt 12:46–50; Mk 3:31-35; Lk 8:19–21). For Lubich, these episodes show that Mary's physical senses may have influenced her thoughts so that they

---

23. Ibid., p. 26.

24. Lubich, "Mary, the Flower of Humanity" in *Essential Writings*, p. 137.

25. Cerini, "The Reality of Mary in Chiara Lubich," p. 27.

26. Ibid.

"might not have been in unison with those of Jesus."[27] These snapshots provide glimpses into how Mary's life with Jesus matured in terms of detachment and rediscovery. They not only prepared her for the supreme detachment she would have to live at the foot of the cross, but they also Christified her way of seeing things, bringing her to the point where she, more than any other human being, could say: "It is no longer I who live, but it is Christ who lives in me" (Gal 2:20). Jesus, out of love for his mother, used these occasions to raise "Mary to the 'greatness' of God the Father."[28] Mary, by silencing her way of seeing things and submitting herself to her Son's will, entered into a deeper recognition of God as the Father of Jesus, of her and of all humanity. In moving from the role of mother to that of sister, Mary shows how to share in the gift of filiation that her son lives vis-à-vis the Father.

She, in whom love became incarnate, is a bridge between the creator and all of creation, between the divine and the human. As mother of the uncreated, Mary shows created beings how to "create," how to generate "the presence of Jesus in the midst" and so give "Jesus to the world spiritually," as she "did physically."[29] Mary, as the mother of love, most copies God-Love and so can best teach us how to love, how to open our hearts to all those who thirst for her Son, how to soothe their pains, close their wounds and dry their tears.

---

27. Lubich, "And the Focolare Was Born" in *Essential Writings*, p. 50.
28. Lubich, *Mary: The Transparency of God*, p. 92.
29. Ibid., p. 57.

Mary Desolate

For Lubich, Jesus' words: "Woman, here is your son" (Jn 19:26) mark the moment of Mary's desolation. Having been asked by God to be the mother of his Son it seems that Mary was now being asked to return to God the gift of her divine maternity and to replace it with the motherhood of John. To Mary, these words must have sounded like a substitution. She whose spiritual journey had brought her relationship with God from a vertical "I-God" to a horizontal "I-Jesus-God" was being asked to relinquish her unique experience of God in Jesus for a seemingly ordinary human relationship with John. Wanting only what her Son wanted, Mary metaphorically raised herself up onto his cross, from which she transferred herself into the heart of John. In other words, she who had lovingly followed Jesus interiorly to the point of participating in his forsakenness became a transparent image of her Son and, as such, "another Jesus." As the first "actualized" Christian, the first to be in complete union with Jesus, Mary gave herself as a spiritual mother to John and, in him, to every human being. Thus it can be said that in her desolation Mary paradoxically facilitated her Son's forsakenness and embodied its salvific goal. She who had "lost" God in Jesus found him again, many times over, in John. Here Lubich's words serve to bring into relief God's design of love on Mary, and in her on every person: "Our inner life is fed by our outer life. The more I enter into the soul of my brother or sister, the more I enter into God within me. The more I enter into God

within me, the more I enter into my brother or sister.
God — myself — my brother or sister."[30]

On the cross Jesus brought all humanity onto a
par with himself, thus providing "some insight into
our potential greatness as human beings. Each of us
is truly destined to be another Jesus, to be divine, in
some way as he is."[31] As the first human being to be
transformed into "another Jesus," Mary personifies
a new kind of person, no longer an individual but a
person-communion. Enabled by the grace of God to
empty herself and move beyond her exclusive love
for her Son, Mary co-generates another Christ in John
and in so doing gathers all human beings into herself.
Through this self-sacrificing act Mary appears as the
bond and mother of unity.

Keeping in mind the essential distinction between
the divine and the human, Lubich draws a parallel
between Jesus' forsakenness and Mary's desolation.
God, through Jesus Forsaken, redeems humanity.
Mary, by accepting John as her son, fuses her desolation with that of her forsaken Son "for the redemption
of the human race."[32] In her the paradoxical purpose
of suffering can be seen: "Unless a grain of wheat falls
into the earth and dies, it remains just a single grain;
but if it dies, it bears much fruit" (Jn 12:24). Lubich's
understanding of Mary Desolate as the one who
"shared Jesus' abandonment and accepted the loss of
her Son *for us*"[33] highlights the inseparable reciprocity

---

30. Lubich, "A God Who Is Love" in *Essential Writings*, p. 65.

31. Lubich, *Mary: The Transparency of God*, p. 42.

32. Lubich, *Mary: The Transparency of God*, p. 64.

33. Lubich, *When Our Love Is Charity*, p. 134.

between one's personal identity and the saving func-
tion, between one's being and the expression of that
being in love of God and neighbor. "Dying" to her
exclusive love for Jesus, Mary exemplifies a love that
transforms suffering, that generates a life of communion, that "places us in God and God is Love."[34] She
who had given physical life to Jesus now completes
God's plan for her by giving spiritual life to all the
members of his mystical body, the Church. Having
given his mother to John, Jesus turns to his beloved
disciple and says: "Here is your mother" (Jn 19:27).
The Gospel of John continues: "And from that hour
the disciple took her into his own home." For Lubich,
the fact that John took Mary home means that every
Christian must take Mary home, to live with her, to go
to Christ with her and through her. On the cross, in
the moment of redemption, Jesus gave his mother to
the whole of humanity in John. There is no other way
to take full advantage of redemption than to do the
will of Jesus, that is, to take Mary home and through
her to reach Jesus. In giving back to God the very thing
that had made her unique, her divine maternity, Mary
Desolate models how individual and collective egos
can be immolated. In her desolation Mary shows herself to be the utmost expression of what Lubich calls
"the negative virtues" — "meekness par excellence,
gentle, poor to the point of losing her Son who is God
… the righteous one who does not complain when
deprived of what was given her purely by election; the
pure one in emotional detachment … the strong one

34. Lubich, "The Art of Loving" in *Essential Writings*, p. 84.

who endured."[35] She is the queen of all the virtues
adorned with purity, patience, temperance, prudence,
justice and above all with charity. Detached from all
that is not God, Mary is no longer defined simply by
her sorrows. Because of her cooperative effort in the
history of salvation, Mary is now defined as the first
human being to have been transformed into Christ.
As the fullest expression of her Son's redeeming
work, the Desolate is, for Lubich, "certainty of sanctification, the perennial font of union with God, a cup
overflowing with joy."[36] In her the human vocation is
completely fulfilled.

Mary Desolate: Model for Women

God, who called Mary to be the mother of his
Son and who raised her to the fullness of perfection
beneath the cross, in her raises all women to
extraordinary levels of dignity. Every woman who
has ever sought to have her self-worth recognized
and her rights affirmed will discover in Mary "what
she should be, her equality with men and her true
identity."[37] In the family "she too can have a leading
role" and "go beyond the family circle in order
to share her unique gifts for the good of many."[38]
Lubich believes, however, that women who reach

---

35. Lubich, "The Charism of Unity and the Media" in *Essential
    Writings*, p. 300.

36. Lubich, "Mary, the Flower of Humanity" in *Essential Writings*, p. 139.

37. Lubich, "The Family: Treasure Chest of Love" in *Essential Writings*,
    p. 182.

38. Ibid.

these legitimate goals do not necessarily feel fulfilled; they need something much deeper in their lives. She maintains that the "whole question surrounding the position of women has its roots in that terrible prophecy announced in Genesis. After the event of original sin and the announcing of the punishment meted out to the man and the woman (to work by the sweat of his brow and to bring forth children in pain), the prophecy says: 'He (the man) shall rule over you' (Gn 3:16)."[39] While it is Christ who redeems all wrongdoing, it is Mary Desolate who shows women how to "discover a Jesus who is alive. And just as in the times when he was physically present," they too will "feel that his love and his message makes them new and whole."[40]

Mary Desolate: Model of a Trinitarian Humanity

Lubich, who believes Christ to be "the way, the model for each one of us,"[41] found herself confronted with the question: "How then can I live Mary?" Using the analogy of being/not being as a way of speaking about what clearly transcends human reason and language, she answers: "By silencing the creature in me, and upon this silence letting the Spirit of the Lord speak. In this way I live Mary and I live Jesus. I live Jesus upon Mary. I live Jesus by living Mary."[42] Thus, in order to model our lives on Christ, and in him on

39. Lubich, "The Talents and Gifts of Women" in *Essential Writings*, p. 196.

40. Ibid., p. 199.

41. Lubich, *The Cry of Jesus Crucified and Forsaken*, p. 18.

42. Lubich, "Mary, the Flower of Humanity" in *Essential Writings*, p. 138.

the Trinity, we must, according to Lubich, embody Mary. We must be a continuation of her.[43]

The doctrine of the Immaculate Conception, Mary being born sinless, raises a question: how can a sinful and fallen humanity be like her? Though not born immaculate, human beings can be like Mary simply because in baptism God pours his very self into them and continuously renews them in the Eucharist.[44] Karl Rahner clarifies this point:

> For us too [God] eternally intended this saving grace from the beginning, in his eternity, even though it was only effected in us after the beginning of our earthly, temporal life, in order that it might be plain that it is all his grace, that nothing in our salvation belongs to us of ourselves. God has eternally kept his eternal love in readiness for us too, so that in the moment that we call our baptism, he may come into the depths of our heart. For we too have been redeemed. We too have been made the holy temple of God. In us too the triune God dwells."[45]

God chose Mary to communicate his triune self to humanity. She, by confidently entrusting herself to him and accepting his outpouring of love, is the most perfect realization of free submission in faith. She teaches how to live "not only according to the model

---

43. Lubich, "Mary in the Focolare Movement" in *Essential Writings*, p. 43.

44. "The Sacrament of Baptism" and "The Sacrament of the Eucharist" in *The Catechism of the Catholic Church*.

45. Rahner, *Mary Mother of the Lord*, p. 49.

of the Trinitarian life but also within the interiority of the Trinitarian life."[46]

As the anthropological realization of the total, eternal, unconditional and mutual self-giving lived by the Father and the Son in the Spirit, Mary models how to respond to God's immense love for humanity by offering her entire being to her creator. Immersed in this divine relationship, she shows how to seek the good of the other without any self-interest, how to be spiritual mothers or fathers, always ready to take the initiative in loving the other. Her selfless love for her Son manifests itself in her ever-growing ability to receive love in a detached way. As the mother of Jesus, Mary wants her fellow human beings to experience his presence in the depths of their hearts, to listen to him in the words of God, to acknowledge him in the Eucharist, in those who suffer, in those who represent him, among those gathered in his name (see Mt 18:20) and, especially, as the Forsaken One. She shows how to receive the love of God in a way that will allow the least in society to be welcomed, and any discrimination that may arise from power, race, sex, wealth and culture to be rejected. The apex of Mary's faith-filled response to God's love happened beneath the cross of her Son where her charity, continuously poured into her heart by the Holy Spirit, was purified. Having spent her life as the handmaid of love to Love, Mary is now transformed into Love. As the unique human being upon whom the Holy Spirit descended, whom the Father overshadowed, and in whom the Word became

---

46. Cambon, p. 15.

flesh, Mary demonstrates how to imitate the life of the Trinity and, just as the Father is everything to the Son and the Son is all for the Father, to make a complete gift for the neighbor who is nearest. She wants her fellow human beings to welcome and continually reinforce these divine relationships of love in their lives to the point where they, like her, become "little 'Saviors,' little Christs, little suns, little God-Loves."[47]

Mary Desolate: An Ecclesial Soul

As the first human being to be redeemed by Jesus, Mary is the first to embody the "oneness," the union with God that Jesus prayed for before his passion (see Jn 17:21). As "another Jesus" she recognized and reached out with all her heart in love to Jesus in John. By losing herself in John, Mary, who had given Jesus physically to the world, attracts "the presence of Jesus into the collectivity."[48] Together she and John formed the first Christian community, the first living cell of the mystical body of Christ, with his risen presence in their midst (see Mt 18:20). In taking on the maternity indicated to her by her dying Son, Mary, in some way the synthesis of his mystical body, models how to lose God within for God in the brothers and sisters. As the human-divine mother of God and the spiritual mother to every human being, Mary contains within herself the mystical body of her Son. As such she is best suited to model the love that characterized her

47. Lubich, cited by Cerini in *God Who Is Love*, p. 38.
48. Lubich, "The Charism of Unity and Economy" in *Essential Writings*, p. 288.

Son, a love that seeks the unity of her children with God and each other.

By his living and especially by his dying, Jesus Forsaken shows himself to be the one supreme mediator between God and humanity (see 1 Tim 2:5). As both priest and victim he incarnates a love that is both self-sacrificial and a concrete service to others. Although as a layperson Mary was not able to offer Christ sacramentally to the world she, who more than any other human being united her own sufferings with those of her Son, shows members of the ordained clergy and members of the royal priesthood how to be a living sacrifice in Jesus, how to be truly a *priest*.[49] As the pattern and form of Christ's mystical body, Mary's divinization, constantly at work within her, through the Eucharist, became always fuller and fuller.

In her new role as the mother of the whole of humanity, Mary, with Peter and the other apostles, gathered in the Cenacle, prayed for God's help in bringing her Son's last will and testament to fruition. Within the heart of the newborn Church, Mary, on whom the Holy Spirit had descended many times, was instrumental in generating new life in and among the apostles so that their faces, words, actions, indeed the whole of their beings were transformed into living witnesses of God's advent in them and among them.

In Mary, the Church finds a woman who put her faith into practice to the point of feeling herself, at the foot of the cross, abandoned by her God, Jesus. In her,

---

49. Lubich, *The Cry of Jesus Crucified and Forsaken*, p. 33.

"who gave and said the *Word*,"[50] the Church discov-
ers its mission to evangelize. She, whose whole life
was totally focused on the Word, shows how to "be
nothing" so that God can speak his Word in and
through the members of the Church to all humanity. Through her act of reaching out to Jesus in John,
Mary acts as a guide for all who seek to radiate Christ
in their daily lives, thereby bringing the whole world
back to God. She whose greatness consisted in focus-
ing on Christ, following him and searching him out,
can help direct the Church in its pastoral outreach, its
ecumenical dialogue with other Christian Churches,
with the faithful of other religions and with all people
of good will. By imitating Mary in her desolation, the
Church can enter into the darkness experienced by
those who feel themselves separated from God and,
like her, they too can be instruments of unity, helping everyone discover and rediscover the Father's
immense love for them.

Immersed in the Trinitarian logic of mutual love,
Mary shows how to foster that level of mutual love
asked by Peter of the first Christian community:
"Above all, maintain constant love for one another"
(1 Pet 4:8). The Church, itself a reality immersed in
the Trinity, can learn from Mary how to attract souls,
inflame hearts, and so help each one and all together
live this Trinitarian dynamic of love. She teaches the
Church how to go to God with and through others
and so be a "people united in the unity of the Father,

---

50. Lubich, "Queen of the Apostles" in *Mary, The Transparency of God*,
    p. 99.

the Son and the Holy Spirit."[51] Mary's role as mother of the God-Man, who magnifies the greatness of God and his works, who participated in God's design of universal salvation, and who continuously shares with the Holy Spirit the task of giving Love to the world, points to a Marian way of life lived existentially within the mystical body.

The Work of Mary[52]

The "Work of Mary is the mystical presence of Mary and therefore the heaven of Jesus in our midst."[53] Its statutes were approved by the Church in 1990 with the specific aim of bringing about the unity that Jesus prayed for, "May they all be one," by loving Jesus Forsaken in each neighbor.

Those who live mutual love to the point of becoming other "little Marys," find themselves living with the Spirit of her risen Son in their midst. They discover, in an ever-new way, his presence in them and through them working to activate the life of his mystical body. With Jesus present in them and among them, their work, like that of Mary, has a twofold effect on all who meet them: "that of bearing *witness* ('May they be one in us, so that the world may believe' [Jn 17:21]), and that of offering to them — through their conversion — the possibility of putting unity into effect themselves, to link up with one another as living members of a single

---

51. Vatican II, *Lumen gentium*, n. 4.
52. "The Work of Mary" and "The Focolare Movement" are interchangeable in their meaning.
53. Lubich, cited by Povilus in *United in His Name*, p. 125.

body."[54] This twofold effect produces many and varied fruits among all who with Mary live the various stages of her journey from Nazareth to Calvary. It is the Spirit of the risen Jesus in the midst of people who makes "all things new" (Rev 21:5), who generates a "new humanity" which, in turn, reflects the image of God. Human nature, having been received into the triune love of God, now carries within it the image of this love. It can be lived existentially by those who work with God the Creator to perfect both the natural order and the lives of their fellow human beings, with God the Son through their capacity to receive love in a detached way, and with the Holy Spirit in the reciprocal realization of love.

In order to incarnate the Trinitarian dynamic of love each one must make of themselves a "gift" for the other and live this "giftedness" in ways that enter into and transform society's structures and social projects. Among the many practical applications of this "giftedness" is the Economy of Communion. This is not an exclusively human activity but, as an expression of the Work of Mary, "is, in itself, a Work of God, at least in its spirit and essential aspects."[55]

This is "a unique manifestation of a free economy based on solidarity."[56] The businesses involved in this project "tap their expertise and resources to produce

---

54. Lubich, *The Cry of Jesus Crucified and Forsaken*, p. 92.

55. Lubich, "Four Aspects of the Economy of Communion" in *New Humanity Review* 6.

56. Lubich, "The Charism of Unity and Economy" in *Essential Writings*, p. 274.

together wealth for the benefit of those in need."[57] The profits from these companies are then put in common, one part being used "to help the poor by providing for their needs until they [find] work."[58] Another part is used "to develop structures to form 'new people' ... that is, people formed and animated by love"; and the last part is "used for the growth of the company."[59]

Conclusion

Although Lubich's reflection on the human condition extends into many areas of theology and human experience, it has a unifying core in the Trinity. From the moment of her first "yes," spoken at the Annunciation, Mary was immersed in this Trinitarian life of communion and its logic of mutual love. Contained within, and containing within herself the triune God, Mary Desolate is, according to Lubich, the model of what it is to be human, of what it is to be another Jesus.

Informed by the biblical figure of Mary, Lubich sees the different stages of Mary's life as signposts along a spiritual path interspersed with joy, sorrow, light and shade until, eventually, those who follow it with all their being are brought into a glorious union with God. This union is found within, in the individual, and without, among two or more gathered in his name (see Mt 18:20). Lubich uses every stage of Mary's journey to emphasize not only the privileges that rightly belong to this unique creature, but also those aspects of her

---

57. Ibid., p. 275.
58. Ibid.
59. Ibid.

life that make it possible for her children to imitate her and so to live the gospel message of love with ever greater perfection. She who put God before all else in her life shows how to love God, how to belong entirely to him with total love, time, energy and intellect. By putting her faith into action in a continuous act of obedience to God, Mary shows human beings how to express their love for God with their neighbors. As a lifelong contemplative, Mary shows how to "lose" one's individual will in order to bring "into full relief and power the reality of being Church."[60]

As an anthropological model, Mary demonstrates how to assimilate the words of God "one by one until they penetrate the depths of our souls and become almost the substance of our being, the new mindset of the 'new self' in us."[61] As a living word of God she shows what it means to be in another, to act as Another who lives within, to find freedom in freedom from self, from one's shortcomings, from one's non-being.[62] In her, humanity's Trinitarian vocation and transcendent destiny reaches its fulfillment. United to her Son, and in him to the Father and the Spirit, Mary is mystically present in each one and among one another. She is the access point for the Christian community to contemplate the triune mystery that opens up in Christ. Wanting only the unity for which her Son prayed, Mary shows how to live the Word,

---

60. Coda, "Reflections on Theological Knowledge" in *An Introduction to the Abba School*, p. 47.

61. Lubich, "The Word That Gives Life" in *Essential Writings*, p. 127.

62. Ibid.

God's will, participation in Christ's salvific event, and its transmission among all God's people. In making of herself a gift for Jesus in John, Mary models the life of communion whereby her interiority is assumed with that of John into that of Christ. It becomes his. Thus Mary shows how to "lose" self out of love and how to "find" self again in the very interiority of God. This transition reflects, according to Giuseppe Maria Zanghí, "the Christian mystery of the resurrection of the flesh" which "includes every man and woman with whom I have communion."[63]

After this brief outline of Lubich's experience and thought on Mary Desolate as an anthropological model, Lubich's "The Invitation of Mary" can be used to illuminate all of the above.

The Invitation of Mary

May she who made God the ideal of her life, help us to make him the ideal of ours, as well.

May she who made the will of God her own at the incarnation and throughout her life, help us fulfill it to perfection.

May she who loved her neighbor, as the episodes of her visit to St. Elizabeth and of the wedding feast of Cana show, fill our hearts with this love.

May Mary, who lived mutual love to the fullest in the family of Nazareth, help us to put it into practice as well.

---

63. Zanghí, "From the 'interior castle' to the 'exterior castle', " p. 26.

May Mary, who knew how to offer every suffering at the foot of the cross, fortify our hearts when suffering will come.

May Mary, who is the mother of all, help us to have a heart that embraces all of humanity.

Even if our planet is plagued by strife and tension, she urges humankind towards unity. In every sense she desires it.

She wants families to be united, the different generations to be united.

She desires unity among races, nationalities, among Christians, as much as possible among members of different religions, and at least on an operative level, with all those seeking the good of humankind.

She loves all humanity and desires universal brotherhood. With her, the first layperson of the Church, we laypersons can rise to the challenge that the Church calls for today: to work for our sanctification, which is the universal vocation of all humanity, to contribute to renewing and expanding the Church, and to give a Christian soul to the affairs and endeavors of the world surrounding us. May it all be for the glory of God and of his mother.[64]

---

64. Chiara Lubich, "The Invitation of Mary" in *Living City*, 27/8-9 (1988), p. 3.

4

An Evaluation of Chiara Lubich's Notion of Mary Desolate as an Anthropological Model in the Focolare Movement

Introduction

Of the many unique elements that comprise Lubich's spirituality of unity, this chapter will begin with a brief evaluative look at what she has called "The Three Communions" — The Word, The Eucharist, and Mutual Love. This will be followed by an assessment of Lubich's thought in regard to Jesus Forsaken. It will conclude by exploring, against this background, the anthropological implications of Mary in her desolation at the foot of the cross[1] for the members of the Focolare Movement and, consequently, for the Church.

---

1. Fabio Ciardi, in an overview of the various spiritualities that have given life to the Church throughout the centuries, perceives in Lubich's spirituality of unity, "the advent of a Copernican revolution. Just as it was discovered that it was the earth that went around the sun, not the sun that went round the earth, so with the collective spirituality one experiences that each of our lives revolves around the Trinity and the presence of Jesus in our midst, and in this new lifestyle, the Trinity and Jesus are found within us. It is a true revolution in the Church and in humanity" (*Being One*, 4/2 [1995] p. 14). See also P. Coda, "The Spirituality of Unity in the Christian Vocation" in *Essential Writings*, p. xix. "The truth, novelty and beauty of what Chiara Lubich teaches about spirituality consists — through the breath of the Holy Spirit — in helping to bring about today the light and grace of the unity Christ has realized in human history."

An Evaluation of Lubich's Theology of Unity

Before attempting to evaluate Lubich's theology of unity, it is important to remember that, for Lubich, "the nature of unity is revealed in Trinitarian love" embodied, "brought to earth and made possible in the lives of creatures through the Incarnation, and the 'new' commandment of Jesus: 'As I have loved you, so you also should love one another' (Jn 13:34; 15:12)."[2] The gospel's fundamental message of love, therefore, is a call to unity. It is a call to all human beings to reflect in their daily lives the unity incarnated in Jesus between heaven and earth, between the uncreated and the created. Based on Jesus' new commandment of reciprocal love, Lubich believes that the "fullness of each person coincides with the 'self-emptying' entailed in being wholly for the other."[3] In living wholly for the other, Jesus crucified and forsaken showed himself to be the existential key to building unity through the Word, the Eucharist, and mutual love. Mary, a created being, models the ontological condition of creation itself — a gift with a destiny directed toward God.

The Word

Jesus, "the Word pronounced from eternity by the Father,"[4] is the personal self-communication of the intra-Trinitarian reality God. While remaining fully divine God, for our salvation Jesus went "outside of

---

2. D. Schindler, "Introduction" in *Introduction to the Abba School*, p. 8.
3. Ibid.
4. Lubich, *The Word of Life*, p. 18.

himself"[5] and "became flesh" (Jn 1:14). By embodying God's design of love he showed human beings that "each and every one has been created as a gift for us, and we as a gift for others."[6] The Second Vatican Council's *Pastoral Constitution on the Church in the Modern World, Gaudium et spes,* states: "It is only in the mystery of the Word made flesh that the mystery of man takes on light" (#22). By introducing human beings into the Trinitarian dialogue of divine love, Jesus throws light on the mystery of what being human means. This light *"generates* Christ in our souls and in the souls of others"[7] so that the meaning of humanity is found in Christ and in him, in the Trinity. This began when God, in infinite love for Mary, "emptied himself" (Phil 2:7) into her womb.

The Eucharist

The Eucharist forms the very foundation of Lubich's 1949 mystical experience.[8] According to her, Jesus' prayer

5. Cerini, *God Who Is Love*, p. 70.

6. Lubich, "Jesus Forsaken" in *Essential Writings*, p. 88.

7. Lubich, *The Word of Life*, p. 83.

8. Gerard Rossé, speaking about the pact of unity between Chiara Lubich and Igino Giordani, highlights the link between the Eucharist and mutual love. "Since the eucharist is in its vital reality a sacrament of unity, love lived reciprocally renders it effective in everyday life. By living in unity, believers are inseparably both Church and Christ (while keeping their distinction). An original aspect of this charism emerges: the reality called Soul brings about something that constitutes the Church. More precisely, the text of the pact does not explicitly speak of reciprocal love, but rather of nothingness. This nothingness, however, is not something added on to love as though it were a third element, but expresses instead the quality of the love. Furthermore, this nothingness is not lived as a private relationship with Jesus in the eucharist but in reciprocity with others. Finally, this nothingness has a specific face: Jesus forsaken, who constitutes the quality and the measure of that nothingness" ("The Charism of Unity" in An Introduction to the *Abba School*, p. 58).

for unity "can be lived fully only through the Eucharist, which makes us not only one through love, but one body and one blood with Christ and with each other."[9] These words are reflected in *Lumen gentium*, 26: "The sharing in the body and blood of Christ has no other effect than to accomplish our transformation into that which we receive."[10] For John Paul II, because Mary's whole life shows her to be a "woman of the Eucharist," the members of Christ's Mystical Body are called "to imitate her in her relationship with this most holy mystery."[11]

Having received the body and blood of Christ in her womb, Mary became the first member of the royal priesthood to give Christ to the world. Lubich, citing Hans Urs von Balthasar, asserts that the dying Jesus "gives his mother communion in the cross (he gives his mother a cross like his own), because he withdraws himself from her, as the Father withdraws himself from the Son."[12] Thus comes about a remarkable synthesis between Mary, who gave the physical presence of Christ to the world, and the Eucharist, which gives Christ's

---

9. Lubich, *A New Way*, p. 62. See also Norris, *A Fractured Relationship*, p. 193, who reiterates this point: "The effect of the Eucharist is that the eternal life of the Father given to the Son in the 'heart' of the blessed Trinity arrives in human hearts. The result will be that human hearts will arrive in the bosom of the Father, being placed there by the Eucharistic Heart and beside the Eucharistic Heart."

10. St. Leo, Martyr, *Serm.* 63, 7: *PL* 54, 357C.

11. See the sixth chapter of John Paul II's encyclical letter *Ecclesia de Eucharistia* (2003), n. 53, "At the School of Mary, 'Woman of the Eucharist.' "

12. H. U. von Balthasar, "Mysterium pascale" in *Mysterium Salutis* (Brescia, 1971) IV: 272-273. Cited by Lubich in *The Cry of Jesus Crucified and Forsaken*, p. 112.

mystical yet real presence under the appearances of bread and wine.

Mutual Love

In a world that often promotes the "I" over the "we," Lubich stresses the collective, communitarian, reciprocal and mutual understanding of love grounded in the very nature of the Trinity.[13] Her spirituality of unity is characterized by the belief that a "triune God shares divine life with the created world calling us to care for one another in a manner similar to the inner dynamics of the trinitarian life."[14] Lubich's teaching reflects not only the teachings of the Second Vatican Council, especially its enunciation of collegiality, but also finds an echo among some philosophers, such as Martin Buber, who examine the nature of dialogue. Although he confines his thought to the physical world, Buber maintains that the I "exists only through the relation to the Thou."[15] Gabriel Marcel's reflection on the human condition summons an awareness of the mystery of being. For him, the development of the individual in person-to-person dialogue is paramount.[16] In the same vein, Lubich's insight that a Christian goes to God through others sheds fresh light on the com-

13. Povilus explores Lubich's understanding of this theme throughout *United in His Name*. In *Reason Informed by Faith*, p. 65, R. M. Gula characterizes the Trinity as "the theological code word for the freedom and totality of God's self-giving."

14. R. F. Morneau, "Preface" in Povilus, *United in His Name*, p. 8.

15. M. Buber, *Between Man and Man*, p. 205.

16. See G. Marcel: www.philosophyprofessor.com/philosophers/gabriell-marcel.php.

munitarian life that the Church wants to bring about during this particular historical moment.

Chiara Lubich's discovery of a God who is love, a God who calls humanity to live in the manner of the Trinity, is reflected in the "return from exile" of Trinitarian theology[17] within recent Catholic theology. This, in turn, has resulted in a new exploration of the anthropological and ecclesial relevance of the Trinitarian paradigm.[18] The tendency in modern Western thought to set the subject against the objects has resulted in Nietzsche's "death of God" and Heidegger's "loss of being." Lubich's understanding of a God who

---

17. For example, see Forte, *The Trinity as History*.

18. J. Castellano, "Letter to Chiara Lubich, 21 June 1992" cited by C. Lubich in A New Way, p. 20. Contrasting the difference between "individual" spiritualities and the Focolare spirituality of unity, he maintains that Lubich's communitarian and ecclesial characteristics make it "a hallmark of our century, where there has been a rediscovery of the Church." He also says that throughout history no other Christian spirituality has reached the point of saying that "as is the case in the Focolare, 'If the Trinity is in me and in you, then the Trinity is among us, we are in a Trinitarian relationship.... Therefore our relationship is in the image of the Trinity; indeed, it is the Trinity that lives this relationship in us.' " See also Miloslav Cardinal Vlk, "Preface" to Lubich, *A New Way*, p. 10. He maintains that Lubich's existential understanding of the Christian revelation of the triune love of God is useful in entering "always more fully into the Trinity's way of being — that is, into communion." See also S. Cola, "The Church in Dialogue" in *Being One* 6/2 (1997), p. 65: "We know that if God is a Trinity of Persons, then theoretically only a society which lives 'like the Trinity' can be healthy, satisfying, and capable of exalting each human person and all of humankind without distinction and without giving rise to forms of power, abuse or oppression. But if we say this only theoretically by way of short-circuit deduction without it being mediated by experience, then we'll continue to preach a dualistic and dichotomy-type heresy, be it spiritual or Manichean, which is contrary to the Incarnation of Word in Jesus."

is love opens up the possibility "of being lifted up into the movement of the Trinitarian life."[19]

Jesus Forsaken

Each era of theological thought has understood the mystery of Jesus' forsakenness in its own fashion. The deep reality of the forsaken Christ remained unexplored, however, until the first half of the 20th century when theologians began to enter into this mystery more courageously and to draw out from its depths profound scriptural teaching.[20] Although not referring specifi-

---

19. Norris, *The Trinity*, p. 165.

20. As early as 1944 Lubich had understood Jesus Forsaken as "the 'something more' *of* the Passion and in the Passion" (*A New Way*, p. 51). In him she saw a love capable of losing God for God. See also Zanghí, "Towards a Theology of Jesus Forsaken," p. 57. He states that through this insight "a new highpoint is offered to the spiritual life, a night which goes beyond the night of the senses and of the spirit, the night of God. God in himself lost for the God who is or who awaits being born in our brothers and sisters!" See also Hemmerle, "Tell me about your God," pp. 19–20, who notes that this "is the originality *par excellence* of Chiara's experience of God…. This goes far beyond a theology which treats only of truths and commandments, although I don't want to take from that. Here we find something different: a new comprehension of the mystery of God." In *The Cry of Jesus on the Cross*, Gerard Rossé, reflecting Lubich's thought, says that this "implies the courage of knowing how to lose one's own certainty of 'possessing him' in order to make a space for one's brother to find him" (p. 124). See also Blaumeiser, "Jesus Forsaken and the Church," p. 9, which outlines three ways that Jesus Forsaken can be considered as the meeting point between God-Trinity and humanity: "1. Through Jesus Forsaken, humanity enters into the Trinity: the Church as communion of saints, as the One gathered in the bosom of the Father. 2. Through Jesus Forsaken the Trinity 'goes out' as it were from itself and reaches the whole of humanity: the Church as universal plan of salvation. 3. In Jesus Forsaken the people of God finds its decisive form and key for realizing its mission: the Church as the instrument of unity of humanity with God and among themselves."

cally to Jesus Forsaken, J. Maritain claims that suffering "exists in God in an infinitely more real manner than it does in us, but without imperfection, because in God suffering is in absolute unity with love."[21] For von Balthasar, "The inarticulate cry of the cross of Jesus is no denial of his articulate proclamation to his disciples and to the people ... instead it is the final end of all those articulations ... which he utters with the greatest force where nothing articulate can be said any longer."[22] In every age each Christian tradition has sought to understand the mystery of suffering within the person of Jesus Christ.[23] These understandings, however, have been primarily individualistic. Based on her belief that in his forsakenness Jesus lost God in himself for God in humanity (see Mk 15:34; Mt 27:46),

---

21. J. Maritain, *Approches sans entraves. Scritti di filosofia cristiana* (Rome, 1978) II:291, cited by Lubich in *The Cry*, p. 25.

22. H. U. von Balthasar, *Il tutto nel frammento* (Milan, 1990), pp. 247-49, cited by Lubich in *The Cry*, p. 44.

23. For a Roman Catholic perspective see Paul VI's "The Way of the Cross" in *Insegnamenti di Paolo VI* (1964) 11:212: "Christ not only shows the dignity of pain, he initiates the vocation to pain. He calls pain to come forth from its despairing uselessness, to become a positive source of good when united to his." See also John Paul II's letter on the meaning of human suffering, *Salvifici doloris*, n. 18. Benedict XVI's encyclical *Deus caritas est* states that Jesus' "death on the Cross is the culmination of that turning of God against himself in which he gives himself in order to raise man up and save him. This is love in its most radical form" (n. 12). For an Orthodox perspective see Olivier Clément's *On Human Being*: "By his self-abasement, his degradation, his passion, his dying the death of the accursed, Christ accepts into himself all hell, all the death of the fallen world, even the terrible accusation of atheism (p. 146). Other Christian perspectives can be found in J. Moltmann's *The Crucified God*, which echoes the Reformed tradition of emphasising Jesus' cry of forsakenness on the cross (Mk 15:34). See also M. Bulgakov's *The Lamb of God*; and Reid Isaac's *Conversations with the Crucified*.

Lubich maintains that every level of human suffering, once it is united with Jesus Forsaken, becomes part of the great history of salvation.[24]

Rather than simply emphasizing the negativity of the cross, Lubich's theology serves to rediscover the centrality of the resurrection theme in Christology. For Lubich, there is an intimate link between Jesus Forsaken, found in every form of suffering, and Jesus resurrected, found wherever two or more are gathered together in his name (see Mt 18:20). The same Jesus is loved in every experience of suffering and celebrated in every experience of resurrection.

According to Jesús Castellano, Lubich's spirituality of unity must be measured not against the individual demands of Christian perfection, but against the very goal of the spiritual life of the three divine Persons. This communitarian holiness is an ecclesial holiness with a Trinitarian stamp.[25]

Mary Desolate in the Focolare Movement

"Mary is the model of every member of the Focolare because, as hers was the primary role of being the mother of the physical Christ, the Focolare — as we have seen — has as its most essential role that of bringing into the world ... the spiritual presence of Christ among people today."[26]

---

24. See also Foresi, *Reaching for More*, p. 101. Here he observes: "We see in [Jesus Forsaken's] experience of abandonment the perfect example of the suffering through which the human race was redeemed."

25. Castellano, "Introduction" in *Unity and Jesus Forsaken*, p. 13.

26. From "The Ideal of Unity," a talk given by Chiara Lubich in 1978 (published only in Italian).

Mary became the spiritual mother of her son's mystical body at the foot of the cross when, in making a complete gift of herself to God, she "lost" God in Jesus for God in John. So that "the Spirit of Christ can manifest himself in the greatest degree of purity and fullness" that our "human limits allow,"[27] Lubich believes it essential that the members of the Focolare "know how to lose." Only by losing their personal attachments, their individual points of view and subjectivism, can they make of themselves complete gifts to God in and through each neighbor.

The charism of unity does not reveal new truths, but it does renew what already exists, namely humanity's unity with Christ in the Trinity. Mary's journey of faith toward Calvary, lived as one free and intelligent "yes," reached its apex at the foot of the cross. In her desolation, through her unique "participation in her Son's abandonment, she reached full identification with him"[28] and thus with the entire Trinity. Lubich's charism of unity, therefore, not only maintains solid continuity with tradition but also articulates an authentic strand of it, a strand often neglected. This spirituality is in no way sentimental or superficially consoling; neither can it be confused with any form of regressive pietism. Rather, it calls its members to live the full radicalism of the Christian message in today's world in the way modeled by Mary Desolate.

This way of imitating and, in a certain way, re-living Mary in giving Jesus spiritually to the

27. Rossé, "The Charism of Unity in the light of the Mystical Experience of Chiara Lubich" in *An Introduction to the Abba School*, p. 59.

28. Cerini, "The Reality of Mary in Chiara Lubich," p. 23.

world, is informed by the mystical intuition Lubich experienced in 1949. Her insight concerning Mary "all dressed in the Word of God" and so the "personification" of the scriptures has been, and continues to be, a source of great joy to Evangelicals (understood here as those Protestant Christians who stress justification through faith and the supreme authority of the Bible) who are linked to the Movement. Lubich saw Mary as "a rare and unique creature within the Trinity," and so understood "that what characterized Mary, though in her unique perfection, should characterize every Christian: to repeat Christ, the Truth, with the personality given to each by God."[29] Support for Lubich's view can be found in the ecumenical document signed by scholars from the Roman Catholic, Orthodox, Anglican, Lutheran, Reformed and Baptist Churches, which acknowledges agreement among the various Christian traditions that Mary should be imitated.[30]

Lubich's insights suggest a new and rich Mariology[31] whereby Mary, "Mother of the Son ...

---

29. Lubich, "Mary in the Focolare Movement" in *Essential Writings*, p. 40.

30. See footnote 10 in *Being One* 4/1 (1995), p. 12. The Second Vatican Council's insertion of its document on Mary into its Constitution on the Church encouraged deeper reflection not only on the link between Mary and the Church, but also on Mary as a model to be imitated.

31. Cerini, "The Reality of Mary in Chiara Lubich," pp. 19–22. Here she states that Lubich's "Mariology is not just one area of her theology ... it is a vision of the One from the One ... a unitarian vision of all reality both created and uncreated which is one from the perspective of Mary.... In this Mariology, Mary is seen not so much in her connection with one or other of the central elements of our faith, not only in her relationship with Christ and the Church as Vatican II significantly points out. Rather, Mary is seen in light of the global plan of God for all humanity and for the entire cosmos."

daughter of the Father and the temple of the Holy Spirit,"[32] continues to be mystically present in those who model their lives on her. In them and through them she continues to generate, through the power of the Holy Spirit, the triune presence of God on earth.

Chiara Lubich's anthropology derives from her belief that Jesus Forsaken introduces human beings into the heart of God-Love, a Trinitarian God where each of the divine persons "is by not being."[33] She does not confine this belief to the realm of concepts, but uses it to inform and illuminate life.[34] In opening human intelligence to a new way of thinking in all the areas of theology, Mariology, and anthropology,[35]

---

32. *Lumen gentium*, #53.

33. In "A Few Notes on Jesus Forsaken" in *An Introduction to the Abba School* (p. 90), Zanghí observes that, for Chiara Lubich, "Love, as it is revealed in the Trinity, is Being completely given in the dynamics of the Divine Persons. But since these dynamics are perfect communion in that atemporal instant that is eternity, we need to conclude that Being absolutely is.... In God, One and Triune, then, Being and Non-Being express the reality of Love, without being confused one with the other, but being one in the other."

34. In "Theological Presuppositions towards a Catholic vision of Mariology," pp. 123–24, Hemmerle discusses the ontological realization of being human through being in the other. He highlights how Mary, especially in her desolation, reveals the truth of this claim.

35. Leahy echoes Lubich's thought in saying that "Mary is the radical concretisation of what baptism realises in everyone in the Church of Christ: 'It is no longer I who live but Christ who lives in me (us)' (Gal 2:20). And in Christ we find ourselves in the bosom of the Father. Our 'living space' in the Trinity. God loves us so immensely that he makes himself nothing before us in order to bring us to share in his triune life.... Through grace, God really has brought his 'neighbour' (creation and humanity personified in Mary) on to a par with himself, bringing his 'neighbour' to share in his own life, and thereby making us all neighbours to one another, neighbours who contain one another and neighbours who are responsible for each other." See "Mary, Model of the Church," in *Mary for Earth and Heaven*, pp. 303–04.

Lubich has addressed a fundamental problem — the fracture between Christian thought and life.

In his forsakenness, Jesus incarnated the reality of "being" through his "non-being" on the cross.[36] In her desolation, knowing how "to lose God in Jesus for God in John," Mary was the first human being to experience the in-breaking of a new creation, a new destiny. As Jesus' first disciple, she makes visible the first fruits of his redemption.[37] In becoming the mother of all at the foot of the cross (see Jn 19:26), Mary models what it is to be created in the image of a triune God.[38] She also shows that this reality of being, this reality of participating in the triune life of God, is lived in and through the risen presence of Jesus in our midst (see Mt 18:20).[39]

In presenting Mary as the model for realizing the Christological dimension of Saint Paul's words, "All are one in Christ Jesus" (Gal 3:28), Lubich highlights Jesus' mother as his first disciple, who demonstrates the form of life that emerges from her Son's death and resurrection — Trinitarian communion. Seeing in Mary a model for all human beings, Lubich has succeeded in showing that the power of Jesus' risen presence "makes us Mary, [who] makes us the Work of

---

36. See *Gaudium et spes*, #22.

37. See Leahy, "Mary, Model of the Church" in *Mary for Earth and Heaven*, pp. 300-13.

38. Lubich's proposing Mary Desolate as a model of Trinitarian humanity is consistent with the doctrine of the Theotókos and with the teaching of *Lumen gentium* #53, which highlighted Mary's relationships with the three divine Persons.

39. Povilus, *United in His Name*, p. 126. Here the author cites Lubich's diary entry of June 3, 1967: "Jesus in our midst … is the spiritual return of Christ among a group of his disciples, and therefore in the Church."

Mary."[40] In this role, as "The Work of Mary," Focolare members live the reality of Christian discipleship in its ecclesial dimension.

Mary Desolate: Model of the Church in the Focolare Movement

Just as the Christ event immersed the humanity of Mary completely in the Trinity, so too the reality of the Church is, as *Lumen gentium*, 4 confirms, immersed in the Trinity. As an icon of the Trinity, the Church "is a mystery of communion and sacrament of unity (see LG 1) and needs, as John Paul II affirms, "to respond with particular ardor and urgency to the original personal and ecclesial vocation: to form, in Christ, 'one heart and one soul' (Acts 4:32)."[41]

Seeing Mary Desolate[42] as "the synthesis of the Mystical Body, a little Church that stands before Jesus who is the head of the Church,"[43] Lubich highlights how Mary lives the Word to the point of becoming the living word, that is, where individuals no longer live their own selves, "but ... allow God's word to live in

---

40. Ibid. Lubich reiterated this point on many occasions — on February 26, 1964 at Grottaferrata, Italy; to a group of children on August 13, 1963 at Ala di Stura, Italy; and on December 7, 1964 to a group of Evangelical pastors at Nuremberg, Germany.

41. John Paul II, "A Robust Spirituality of Communion," p. 2.

42. Norris & Leahy, *Christianity: Origins & Contemporary Expressions*, p. 204. Here the authors state: "Mary is important as we go about interpreting the Christian message for today. And not just Mary as an individual but all that she stands for in the Church: the existential 'yes' to God, holiness, prophecy, saints and mystics, laity, women, charisms and new ecclesial movements, outreach, social projects and concrete service in bringing the presence of Christ into the world."

43. Lubich, *Essential Writings*, p. 52.

us, Christ (to be) born in us."[44] Mary is the "woman of the Eucharist" who knows how to love her neighbor "to the point of being consumed in unity,"[45] that is, to the point of having the risen presence of Jesus in our midst (see Mt 18:20). In a special way Lubich focuses on Mary's desolation where, in her love for Jesus Forsaken, she demonstrates how to repeat: "In my flesh I am completing what is lacking in Christ's afflictions" (Col 1:24). In modeling how to live the Word, the Eucharist, mutual love, and especially how to love her forsaken Son, Mary Desolate not only reflects the Trinitarian character of Lubich's theological anthropology but also shows how to be disciples so that Christians, like her, can give Christ (spiritually) to the World.

This understanding of Mary and her work provides a background against which the "feminine can be seen as fundamental not only for a complete hermeneutic of the anthropological mystery, but also for a balanced and authentic hermeneutic of the Church mystery."[46] This mystery begins when Christians, like John, take Mary home with them (see Jn 19:27); that is, when they model their lives on Mary the Mother of Unity who wants all her children to be united in her Son.

At the foot of the cross Mary revealed a Church of communion[47] that transcends the dichotomies between

---

44. Lubich, cited by Povilus in *United in His Name*, p. 30.

45. Ibid., p. 31.

46. Coda, "Three Keys for the reading of *Mulieris dignitatem*," p. 19.

47. As such it is one of the many manifestations of the new and original season of mariological reflection taking place in the Church today. This reflection is built primarily on the Second Vatican Council's insertion of a chapter on Mary in *Lumen gentium*, its dogmatic constitution on the Church. Addressing a group of bishops, friends

the teaching Church and the learning Church, between the ministerial priesthood and the royal priesthood, between universal Church and local or particular church, between the institutional Church and the charismatic Church.[48] By underlining the fundamental aspect of love that makes the Church "one," as in the Trinity, Mary presents to the world a Church with a profile both distinctly Petrine and distinctly Marian.[49] Thus Lubich presents Mary's ecclesial mission as one directed outward, away from self, and into the presence of her Son living in the "other," living in the midst of his mystical body.

In addressing a group of bishops who are friends of the Focolare Movement, John Paul II said: "My wish for you is that you be more and more inspired with, and penetrated by, this spirituality (of the Movement) and by a profound love for Mary, in order to be builders of that city of Mary (Mariapolis) which the Church wants to be and ought to be,

---

of the Focolare Movement, John Paul II said that a "renewed proclamation of the gospel can only be coherent and effective if it is accompanied by a robust spirituality of communion" (*L'Osservatore Romano*, 17 February 1995, p. 5).

48. See Schindler, "Institution and Charism," pp. 27–30.

49. See Leahy, *The Marian Profile*. See also Schindler, "Institution and Charism," pp. 27-29, where he maintains that although the spirit of communion is lived out in the Petrine and Marian dimensions of the Church, they need to be lived out in the ordered way revealed in the Trinity itself: "objective (sacramental) holiness always-already presupposes the 'subject(-ivity)' in which is it received and, as it were, is brought to fulfillment; and subjective holiness is always-already (meant to be) ordered from, toward, and by the 'objective' (sacramental) Other. It is in this way that we have a unity without confusion, and a distinction without separation, between the Petrine-institutional and the Marian-charismatic dimensions of the Church."

in order to carry like Mary and with Mary the light of Jesus Christ into the world of today."[50]

Conclusion

The theology, Mariology, and anthropology of Chiara Lubich form parts of a unified whole. Individually and all together they reflect the main mysteries of the faith seen from the perspective of the Calvary experience of Jesus Forsaken and Mary Desolate. The key hermeneutic for Lubich's theology, Mariology, and anthropology, however, is not confined only to Calvary but encompasses the whole paschal mystery. Within this mystery lies the triune God who shares divine life with the whole of humanity and calls for a human response in a reciprocal love similar to the inner dynamics of the Trinitarian life, a way that generates the presence of the risen Christ in the mystical body. Lubich does not present Jesus Forsaken and Mary Desolate as full expressions of the Christian mystery, but as elements inserted into an overall vision of the Church. For her, Jesus Forsaken and Mary Desolate form a single key to the interpretation of a "realized" community that thousands of her followers have found challenging, enriching, satisfying and awe inspiring.

---

50. John Paul II, *L'Osservatore Romano*, 19 February 1987.

Works Cited

Anonymous. *Didaché.* The Library of Christian Classics, Vol. 1. London: S.C.M., 1953.

Benedict XVI. *Deus caritas est.* (n.12).http://www.vatican.va/ holy_father/benedict_xvi/encyclicals/documents.

Bettenson, Henry. ed., trans., "Cyril of Jerusalem." *The Later Christian Fathers,* Oxford: Oxford University Press, 1977.

Blaumeiser, Hubertus. "Jesus Forsaken and the Church." *Being One* 2/5 (2002).

Buber, Martin. *Between Man and Man.* New York: Macmillan Publishing Co., 1965.

Bultmann, Rudolf. *The Gospel of John: A Commentary.* Oxford: Blackwell, 1971.

Cambon, Enrique. "The Trinity as a Model for Society." *Being One* 4/1 (1995).

Catechism of the Catholic Church. ns. 213, 221. Dublin: Veritas, 1994.

Castellano Cervera, Jesús. "Introduction." *Unity and Jesus Forsaken.* New York: New City Press, 1985.

Cerini, Marisa. "The Reality of Mary in Chiara Lubich." *New Humanity Review* 3 (1998).

____. *God Who Is Love in the Experience and Thought of Chiara Lubich.* New York: New City Press, 1992.

Ciardi, Fabio. "Christian Spiritualities in History." *Being One,* 4/2 (1995).

Clément, Olivier. *On Human Being.* London and New York: New City Press, 2000.

Coda, Piero. "Three Keys for the Reading of *Mulieris dignitatem.*" *Being One* 4/3 (1995).

____. "An Intellectual Biography — Klaus Hemmerle's Unique Contribution as a Philosopher and Theologian." *Being One* 5/1(1996).

____. "Reflections on Theological Knowledge." *An Introduction to the Abba School*. New York: New City Press, 2002.

Cola, Silvano. "New Horizons for Theology and Pastoral Ministry." *Being One* 7/3 (1998).

Downey, Michael, ed., *The New Dictionary of Catholic Spirituality*. Collegeville, MN: The Liturgical Press, 1993.

Egan, Harvey, D. "A Contemporary Mystical Theology." *What Are They Saying about Mysticism?* New York: Paulist Press, 1982.

Foresi, Pasquale. *God Among Men*. London: New City, 1974.

____. *Reaching for More*. Brooklyn: New City Press, 1982.

____. "Choose Wisdom." *Being One* 11/1 (2002).

Forte, Bruno. *The Trinity as History*. New York: St. Paul Publications, 1989.

Gallagher, Jim. *A Woman's Work: Chiara Lubich*. New York: New City Press, 1997.

Giordani, Igino. *Diary of Fire*. London: New City, 1981.

Gula, Richard, M. *Reason Informed by Faith*. New York: Paulist Press, 1989.

Hemmerle, Klaus. "Theological Presuppositions towards a Catholic Vision of Mariology." *Nuova umamità XXI* (1999/3-4).

____. "Tell Me about Your God." *Being One* 5/1 (1996).

John Paul II *Salvifici doloris. n.18.* http://www.vatican.va/holy_father/john_paul_ii/apost_letters/documents.

____. *Dominum et vivificantem n.10.* http://www.vatican.va/holy_father/john_paul_ii/encyclicals/documents.

____. "A Robust Spirituality of Communion." Taken from a talk given to a group of Cardinals and Bishops, friends of the Focolare Movement and published in *Being One* 4/2 (1995).

_____. *Ecclesia de eucharistia. n.53.* http://www.vatican.va/holy _father/special_features/encyclicals/documents.

Johnson, William. *Mystical Theology: The Science of Love.* London: Harper Collins, 1995.

Kasper, Walter. *Jesus the Christ.* London: Burns & Oates, 1976.

Leahy, Brendan. "Mary, Model of the Church." *Mary for Earth and Heaven: Essays on Mary and Ecumenism.* William McLoughlin and Jill Pinnock, eds. Leominster: Gracewing, 2002.

_____. *The Marian Profile in the Ecclesiology of Hans Urs von Balthasar.* New York: New City Press, 2000.

_____. "Il Dio di Maria." *Nuova umanità 26/151* (2004/1).

_____. "To Live the Life of the Trinity — The Eucharistic Invitation." *The Furrow* 56 (2005).

Lossky, Vladimir. *The Mystical Theology of the Eastern Church.* New York: St. Vladimir's Seminary Press, 1976.

Lubich, Chiara. *The Word of Life.* New York: New City Press, 1975.

_____. *The Eucharist.* New York: New City Press, 1977.

_____. "The Invitation of Mary." *Living City,* 27/8-9 (1988).

_____. *A Call to Love.* Spiritual Writings, Vol. 1. New York: New City Press, 1989.

_____. *Fragments of Wisdom.* Mumbai: New City, 1991.

_____. *When Our Love Is Charity.* Spiritual Writings, Vol. 2. New York: New City Press, 1991.

_____. "Collective Spirituality and its Instruments." *Being One* 4/2 (1995).

_____. "For a Philosophy that Stems from Christ." *New Humanity Review* 3 (1998).

_____. "A Doctorate in Education." *New Humanity Review* 5 (2001).

____. *The Cry of Jesus Crucified and Forsaken*. New York: New City Press, 2001.

____. "Love Generates Wisdom." *Being One 11/1* (2002).

____. *Mary: The Transparency of God*. New York: New City Press, 2003.

____. *A New Way*. New York: New City Press, 2006.

____. *Essential Writings*. New York and London: New City Press, 2007.

Marcel, Gabriel. www.philosophyprofessor.com philosophers' gabriell-marcel.php.

Moltmann, Jürgen. *The Crucified God*. London: S.C.M., 1974.

Norris, Thomas. *The Trinity: Life of God, Hope for Humanity*. New York: New City Press, 2009.

Norris, Thomas, and Brendan Leahy. *Christianity: Origins & Contemporary Expressions*. Dublin: Veritas, 2004.

O'Collins, Gerald, and Edward. G. Farrugia. *A Concise Dictionary of Theology*. Edinburgh: T&T Clark, 1997.

Pelli, Anna. "Second Luminous Mystery — The Wedding at Cana: 'Do Whatever He Tells You' (Jn 2:5)." *Contemplating Christ with the Eyes of Mary*. Kildare, Focolare Trust, 2003. Editors Doreen Brady and Maire O'Byrne.

Povilus, Judith, M. *United in His Name: Jesus in Our Midst in the Experience and Thought of Chiara Lubich*. New York: New City Press, 1992.

Rahner, Karl. *Mary Mother of the Lord: Theological Meditations*. London: Herder, 1963.

Ratzinger, Joseph. *Introduction to Christianity*. J. R. Foster, trans. London: Search Press, 1971.

Rossé, Gerard. *The Cry of Jesus on the Cross*. New York/Mahwah: Paulist Press, 1987.

____. "The Charism of Unity in the Light of the Mystical Experience of Chiara Lubich." *An Introduction to the Abba School*. New York: New City Press, 2002.

Sachs, John, R. *The Christian Vision of Humanity.* Collegeville, MN: The Liturgical Press, 1991.

Schindler, David. "Institution and Charism." *Being One 8/1* (1999).

____. "Introduction." *An Introduction to the Abba School.* New York: New City Press, 2002.

Pope Paul VI. *Dei verbum.* n.8; *Lumen gentium.* ns. 53, 58; *Gaudium et spes.* ns. 22, 24; *Perfectae caritatis.* (n.15); *Sacrosanctum concilium.* (n.7); *Apostolicam actuositatem.* (n.18). *Vatican Council II: The Conciliar and Post Conciliar Documents.* New York: Costello Publishing Company, 1975. General Editor Austin Flannery, O.P.

von Balthasar, Hans Urs. *Prayer.* San Francisco: Ignatius, 1986.

____. *Mary for Today.* Middlegreen, Slough: St. Paul Publications, 1987.

____. *The Glory of the Lord: A Theological Aesthetics VII: Theology: The New Covenant.* Edinburgh: T&T Clark, 1989.

Volf, Mirolslav. *Foundations of Christian Faith: An Introduction to the Idea of Christianity.* London: Darton, Longman and Todd, 1978.

Zanghi, Giuseppe, M. "A Few Notes on Jesus Forsaken." *New Humanity Review 1* (1996).

____. "The 'interior castle' to the 'exterior castle' " *Gen's xv 1/2* (2007).

Zizioulas, John, D. *Being as Communion: Studies in Personhood and the Church.* London: Darton, Longman and Todd, 1985.

____. "The Theological Problem of 'Reception.'" *One in Christ 21* (1985), p.1.

Also available:

Essential Writings
Spirituality • Dialogue • Culture
Chiara Lubich

"This selection and arrangement of Chiara Lubich's spiritual writings opens up the heart and soul of one of the most significant religious figures of our times. In our own day, there may be nothing more important than giving witness to the hope and the possibility of unity between and among people of all faiths — and of those with no faith at all. This is the legacy Chiara leaves to everyone concerned with the unity of all people."

Michael Downey, Editor
The New Dictionary of Catholic Spirituality

ISBN 978-1-56548-259-3, paper, 432 pages

Also available:

Chiara Lubich

MARY
The Transparency of God

Mary
The Transparency of God
Chiara Lubich

"It is my hope that these pages of Chiara, so rich in witness to Mary and in meditations about her, may nourish us and help very many people to say like Mary and with her their own 'Here I am,' their own yes to the plan and path that God has prepared for the life of each person. The multitude of people who have walked with Chiara along this path can testify that it leads also by way of the experience of the cross to happiness."

From the Foreword by Joseph Cardinal Schönborn,
Archbishop of Vienna

ISBN 978-1-56548-192-5 , paper, 112 pages